"My good friend and colleague Paul Pettit, and Jason Epps, have done the church of Jesus Christ a great service by writing *One Body, One Spirit: Disability & Community in the Church*. Together they provide a biblically sound and deeply compassionate solution to the problem of churches and ministries being inaccessible to people with disabilities and special needs. Every pastor, youth leader, and ministry professional needs to read this book and implement its principles."

—Mark M. Yarbrough,
President, Dallas Theological Seminary

"Jason and Paul do a great service to God's people by illustrating how to genuinely care for our brothers and sisters in Christ. The steps are simple but they are a path to friendship and greater unity in the body of Christ."

—Patrick Schreiner,
Associate Professor, New Testament and Biblical Theology,
Midwestern Baptist Theological Seminary

"My friends Paul Pettit and Jason Epps have done a great service for the church, for people with disabilities, and for you and me, in writing this much-needed book. It offers a powerful challenge for churches to integrate those with disabilities into their local congregations. This book is not about starting a disability ministry—it is much bigger and better than that. You will love it and, as you will read in the book, 'the finish is worth the start!'"

—Joe Allen,
Campus Pastor, Dallas Theological Seminary

"*One Body, One Spirit* asks Christians tough questions about the social barriers that exist when it comes to befriending a person with a disability. The straightforward action plan offered for all Christians to consider is a definite resource that I will revisit often when evaluating the church's ministry to our disabled community."

—Jacob Hercamp,
Pastor, St. Peter's Lutheran Church

"Here is a book the church has been waiting for. Jason and Paul have given us a clear, compassionate, and hopeful guide toward loving our brothers and sisters well. Pastors and Christian workers will find the Five-Step Plan to be an encouraging framework for faithful action that changes lives."

—Daniel Walbert,
Lead Pastor, Greenhaven Neighborhood Church

"A flood of emotions are running through my emotional arteries because of this book. For the first time in sixty-two years, I am seeing something, though still darkly. I'm seeing how a place I've loved since a little boy sometimes looks to persons with disabilities. How I wish I would have seen this years ago. It's unlike anything I've ever read. And I sincerely pray that Jesus will put his hands on my eyes one more time and help me see your world more perfectly so I can be a better pastor to people with disabilities the last third of my race. Thank you, my brother."

—Mike Holm,
Pastor, Calvary Chapel Tampa

"This book is a must-read, especially for pastors and for anyone feeling shy or inhibited when people with disabilities (PWDs) show up at your church. We often do not know how to treat them, and we certainly don't know what they need, much less know what to say to a PWD. Jason and Paul have presented a masterpiece. They provide many real-life stories as well as a repeatable method on how to treat PWDs. The remedy is simple, but fundamental. Moreover, they write it in real and practical terms because when you talk with people (with or without disabilities), you are conveying dignity and respect. PWDs are no exception. You'll love their stories and their approach."

—Mark L. Hans,
Pastor of Jail and Prison Ministries,
Northwest Community Church

"*One Body, One Spirit* is an outstanding resource for pastors and church leaders seeking a holistic approach to ministry with the largest underserved population by the church in North America—individuals and families impacted by disability. Paul Pettit and Jason Epps blend the unique experiences of a seminary professor with a hidden disability and a community church pastor with a very visible disability in offering a model for welcoming everyone to church—from a person in a wheelchair to a young adult with autism to a family of a child with severe challenges regulating emotions and behavior. Individual Christians moved to share the love of Christ with friends and neighbors impacted by disability will also be inspired and empowered by their ideas and perspectives."

—Stephen Grcevich,
President and Founder, Key Ministry

"I highly recommend this book and will be giving it to pastors and denominational leaders about how to welcome, engage, and involve people with disabilities in their congregations. It's coauthored by two people: one with a physical disability and another with a hidden developmental disability. They share stories from their own experiences, as well as others from people they know. The book is biblically and theologically sound, and provides five steps on how to move forward. May this book help multiply the number of disability-friendly congregations, as well as open the door wider for people with disabilities to enter into leadership roles. The local church is ultimately the best place for individuals affected by disability to be included from cradle to grave. I dream of one day being in a church led by a pastor with a disability."

—Alfonso "Al" Feria,
Founder and CEO, JP's Ability Hope,
Father of a special needs child

ONE BODY, ONE SPIRIT

Disability & Community in the Church

B. JASON EPPS
& PAUL PETTIT

KREGEL
MINISTRY

ISBN 978-0-8254-4792-1

Library of Congress Cataloging-in-Publication Data

Names: Pettit, Paul, 1964– author. | Epps, B. Jason, 1992– author.
Title: One body, one spirit: disability and community in the church / Paul Pettit and B. Jason Epps.
Description: First edition. | Grand Rapids, MI: Kregel Ministry, [2024] | Includes bibliographical references.
Identifiers: LCCN 2024002679 (print) | LCCN 2024002680 (ebook)
Subjects: LCSH: People with disabilities—Religious aspects—Christianity. | Theological anthropology—Christianity.
Classification: LCC BT732.7 .P48 2024 (print) | LCC BT732.7 (ebook) | DDC 259/.44—dc23/eng/20240308
LC record available at https://lccn.loc.gov/2024002679
LC ebook record available at https://lccn.loc.gov/2024002680

Printed in the United States of America

24 25 26 27 28 / 5 4 3 2 1

This book is lovingly dedicated to those who live with ongoing disabilities. May God grant you grace and peace as you face each new day. And we ask the same for all those friends and family who faithfully lend a helping hand.

CONTENTS

ACKNOWLEDGMENTS

We want to thank our research assistants: David Alves, Morgan Underwood, and Autumn Wilson. We appreciate your faithful assistance.

I (Jason Epps) want to express my immense gratitude to everyone who made this work possible. I am grateful for my mother, Christine; my scribe, Amanda Jarus; and my writing partner in this project, Paul Pettit. Where others simply encouraged me to write a book, Paul took the next step by actively helping and guiding me through the entire process.

I (Paul Pettit) thank God for my wonderful wife, Pam, who serves premature babies and their anxious families in one of the world's busiest labor and delivery wards—Parkland Hospital in Dallas, Texas. I also thank God for my friends and colleagues at Dallas Theological Seminary in Dallas, Texas, including my friend and alumnus Jason Epps. And I am especially grateful for those of you accepting the challenge to undertake and implement the Five-Step Plan. May your tribe increase!

INTRODUCTION

Ultimately this book is written for everyone, rather than simply for those already active in disability ministry or those with disabilities. It has been written to foster a mindset among those without a disability to know how best to engage and care for those with disabilities. In short, this book is all about how to develop authentic friendships. This book is a challenge to focus on the individual, rather than the program. We hope that by the time you finish reading it you will be better equipped to follow Jesus's command to love one another.

As a professor of preaching, I (Paul) am accustomed to new students arriving early on the first day. They fidget and squirm, poring over the syllabus with the diligence of a lawyer looking for a loophole. The tension rises as the clock inches closer to the beginning of class. They organize and reorganize their computers, pens, and water bottles as if the perfect alignment might allay their rising anxiety. Unlike the rest of the semester, no one is late on the first day. Except Jason.

That day, I welcomed the fidgeting students and opened in prayer. Soon thereafter, we ran through the attendance to ensure no fresh-faced graduate student had wandered into the wrong room in a syllabus-induced daze. About halfway through, we heard a tapping on the door. As I headed that way to investigate, the door swung open. Was it a lost, fresh-faced graduate student? Two students hovered in the doorway. One stood, holding the door, and the other sat in his powered wheelchair. Unlike most students who wandered in late because they overslept or got caught in Dallas traffic, Jason arrived late because he got stuck in campus traffic—slow elevators, unfamiliar ramp locations, and a heavy classroom door.

Jason's entrance inaugurated a semester-long odyssey into what it is like for a student with a disability to attend graduate school. Our preaching classroom had a stage with a podium, but no ramp. How would Jason get on stage to preach? Would we lower him through the tiled roof like friends lowered the paralytic through the thatch roof? I could not imagine how uncomfortable that would have been for Jason.

I soon realized that, for Jason, details of little significance in my own life—a few inches of elevation and heavy classroom doors—threatened to thwart his ministry. My discussion with Jason about disability in the classroom grew into discussions about disability in the church.

In his experience, the church had not adapted to serve him well. All too often, church staff siloed him into special classes or small groups with others facing disabilities. If you know Jason, you know that his disability is only a sliver of his identity. Yet, instead of grouping him with other young adults, Old Testament scholars, Labrador lovers, or sci-fi enthusiasts, he joined others with disabilities.

Not only had the church failed to serve him well, but many churches refused to be served by him. After class one day, Jason wondered, "Do you believe a church would hire me as their senior minister?" My instinct was immediate affirmation; Jason preached well. Why would a church refuse? Yet, the question lodged itself in my mind like a shard of glass. Over the years, this question has remained. Would a church ever hire a pastor with a disability? A second question was ever sharper: Would my church?

What happens in your church when someone with a disability (like me, Jason) visits? Let us start with physical access. Picture your church in your mind. Does the building have steep stairs and narrow hallways? Do you have spaces in the pews or chairs to accommodate wheelchairs? Would my chair fit through the doorways? How heavy is the front door? Many church buildings are aging and not compatible with the updates required in the Americans with Disabilities Act (ADA) of 1990.

What about social access? Picture your church during a worship service. When someone in a wheelchair rolls through the front door (assuming that it is propped open or a hospitality member has opened it for them), what happens? In my experience, and in the experience of many others, staff and volunteers rush around to accommodate. Whispers fly: "Do we have a special program for this person? Are we equipped for this unique type of outreach? Is anyone here trained in ministry to the disabled?"

Americans with Disabilities Act

The signing of the ADA [Americans with Disabilities Act] was just the beginning of our work toward full acceptance and inclusion of people with disabilities. Even today, many committed clergy and laypeople, both with and without disabilities, continue working to make our communities of faith accessible, not only in terms of physical space, but also in terms of allowing everyone a place to identify their gifts and to put those gifts to use in the service of God.[1]

1. Andy Imparato and Mark Crenshaw, "Faith Communities Provide Access, Inclusion for People with Disabilities," *Medium*, September 19, 2017, https://medium.com/christian-citizen/faith-communities-provide-access-inclusion-for-people-with-disabilities-caf37659ca33.

The flurry of activity when I roll through the front doors is like the subtle commotion when coffee is spilled or the livestream freezes. Whether church leaders realize it or not, the rush reveals that my presence is a problem. Many churches are unaware that their well-intentioned accommodation sends a subtle message: "We're not sure we're ready to undertake ministry to, or in, or with the disability community!"

The church needs constant reminding that all are needed in the body of Christ. Placing our hope in Jesus brings unity amid diversity. We can all experience the joy of oneness without sameness. Each of God's children possesses unique gifts. It's time we receive and embrace the undiscovered gifts offered by those who think in patterns outside the norm. It is never easy, but this book asks you to make an effort to get past the uncomfortable moments along the way.

Hundreds of pastors, staff, and lay leaders in the local church operate from their non-disabled experience. There is a massive deficit in our churches, parishes, and fellowships: an entire category of people is missing. Even as a member of the disability community, I confess that sometimes I have failed to welcome and fully integrate people with disabilities. Yet, insight from Scripture, honesty from those in the disability community, and research from the social sciences reveals a vision of full integration. We will tackle the question of what a fully disability-integrated local faith community might look like. Our hope is to provide a road map for churches to implement this vision and integrate those with disabilities into their local congregations—from pew to pulpit.

OUTLINE

Because Jason and I met during my preaching class, it only seems appropriate to organize this book into a classic sermon outline: problem, solution, and application. Part 1 will explore the issues in the local church as it pertains to including the abilities of all types of people and the barriers experienced by people with disabilities. Chapter 1 invites the reader to explore a typical church gathering through the eyes of someone with a disability. Stairs will no longer be mild cardiovascular exercise; they will be inaccessible walls. Bathrooms will no longer be for small talk. Communion cups will be difficult to hold for those with paraplegia. In the following two chapters, we want to narrow in on the physical and social barriers to full integration, noting research which supports a correlation between facilities, culture, and disinvolvement.

Part 2 moves toward a biblically informed solution to inaccessible churches. Chapters 4 and 5 review disability in the Old and New Testaments and move the reader toward a vision of full integration from pews to pulpit in chapter 6. We will also outline how to conduct a *disability audit,* which allows someone without a disability to see their church facilities and culture from a new perspective for purpose-driven change.

In part 3, we want to move past organizational advocacy and focus on how individual believers can become stewards of a fully integrated gospel community. In this plan we ask a non-disabled person to pray about building an authentic, organic friendship with a person with a disability. Our desire is for the reader to consider praying about personally accepting our disability challenge. Remember, God's heart is *for* people with disabilities. Several addendums will unpack the everyday issues of cross-ability friendships and frequently asked questions about infusing the Five-Step Plan into the DNA of a local church or faith community.

This book is for people with disabilities, those without, and everyone between and along the spectrum. A fully integrated church requires people to be informed, committed, and humble enough to change. Genuine community takes an immense amount of patience, hard work, and grace from both parties.

SCOPE AND TERMINOLOGY

What is a usable definition of disability? The *Oxford Learner's Dictionary* defines disability as "a physical or mental condition that makes it difficult for somebody to do some things that most other people can do."[2] The United Nations Convention on the Rights of Persons with Disabilities defines disability as "long-term physical, mental, intellectual or sensory impairments which in interaction with various barriers may hinder [a person's] full and effective participation in society on an equal basis with others."[3]

Our goal is to encourage readers to fully integrate people with disabilities into faith communities. We want to create exposure for people without disabilities so they can build genuine friendships with people with disabilities, which ultimately spread out into the entire faith community. "Disabled person" and "person with a disability" (PWD) are common terms used by members of the disability community. As a sign of respect for those in this community, we will favor "person with a disability" or "PWD" because the description "disabled person" places their disability as a qualifier of their personhood.

Instead of "able-bodied," we will opt for the term, "person without a disability" or "non-disabled." Throughout this work, those with disabilities

---

2. *Oxford Learner's Dictionary*, s.v. "disability (*n.*)," accessed June 14, 2022, https://www.oxfordlearnersdictionaries.com/us/definition/english/disability.
3. UN General Assembly, *Convention on the Rights of Persons with Disabilities: Resolution Adopted by the General Assembly*, January 24, 2007, A/RES/61/106, https://www.refworld.org/docid/45f973632.html.

may also be termed "assets," and those without disabilities will be termed "handlers" (borrowing from popular spy novels). Our goal of genuine friendships is precisely why we occasionally use the terminology of "asset" and "handler" in this book. "Asset" stresses the value of the person with a disability and "handler" stresses the role of someone who equips them with what they need. The term "friend" or "potential friend" is used to emphasize the ideal end product of the Five-Step Plan, which is mutual friendship.

Many people with disabilities are stuck in an ugly cycle of self-reported worthlessness and doubt. The term "asset" serves as a reminder that PWDs are critical members in faith communities. All are needed in the body of Christ. We continue to employ the terms "disabled" as it has become known in popular culture as someone who has a physical or mental condition that limits their movement, senses, or activities and "disability" as that condition.

We have narrowed the focus of our work primarily toward those with physical disabilities, although we will often include data on those with intellectual and cognitive disabilities as well. The developing field of disability ministry is vast and varied; we decided to narrow the focus of our research to the various experiences in our own lives. In the history of disabilities, change has been ignited when those of us with disabilities have been given a voice. We did not intentionally leave out or overlook a specific physical, mental, or emotional disability. Our intent is to leverage our experiences with data to revolutionize the church.

Every year, churches spend millions of dollars on coffee, livestream cameras, and matching T-shirts—all to cultivate a friendly, welcoming atmosphere. However, thousands of people cannot even make it through the door. People with disabilities face unique challenges when considering local church membership, and most churches are unaware that their ministry programs, speaker systems, and staircases are cultivating a hostile, inaccessible atmosphere. The local church faces a crisis. Can it adapt to serve and be served by *every* Jesus-follower? Or will those with disabilities be left at the door?

MEET YOUR GUIDES

THE ASSET: TRAPPED BETWEEN TWO WORLDS

For most of my life, I (Jason) felt trapped between two worlds. I was born with "spastic quadriplegia." Most people know this as cerebral palsy. Cerebral palsy is one of the broadest disabilities and affects people with various levels of severity. For example, some people with cerebral palsy can walk with a limp. Other people are wheelchair-bound but can communicate verbally. Still others can be wheelchair-bound, verbally uncommunicative, and cognitively impaired. For me, cerebral palsy mostly affects my physical body. My mental faculties are intact, and I can communicate verbally—which is immensely helpful in writing or coauthoring this book since I'm dictating to a scribe!

Growing up with a disability was challenging. I missed playground games like kickball, dodgeball, and baseball. I was relegated to the sidelines. Even off the playground, many of my peers relegated me to the sidelines or avoided me altogether. Whenever I was invited to social events, my wheelchair was often parked in the corner of the room, leaving me far away from conversations. In situations where I could participate, my disability hindered me. Sometimes I would sit there for hours in helpless frustration, wondering why I had attended in the first place.

Occasionally, I had the opportunity to suggest alternative activities, ones where everyone could participate such as board games or trivia. When my ideas were not ignored or dismissed, I felt that my classmates were annoyed their play was limited by my participation. On extremely rare occasions, a well-meaning adult would try to adapt a game so I could participate. If we played a game where students tossed a beanbag into a bucket, the teacher would give me multiple tries and move the bucket closer. Then my peers accused me of cheating. All these situations reinforced my belief that no matter what I did, I could not win. The thought nagged at me: Would it be better for everyone if I were not there? Was my presence a poison, slowly leeching away fun in the "regular world"?

What about in the "disability world," the environment of grade-age peers who all struggled with a disability? In this world, I faced similar problems. When I attended disability camps or all-inclusive activities, I discovered I was one of the few individuals with higher cognitive abilities. Sometimes, the loneliness got to me; there was no one to talk to or interact with. In fact, sometimes the "disability world" felt lonelier than the "regular world" because I constantly felt the pressure that the "disability world" should have felt like home. But it did not.

Churches provided little relief. Many churches I attended had disability ministries geared toward people with severe mental impairments. As someone with a physical disability, I did not fit in. Many of these ministries quarantined me into a "disability district." I felt like we were lepers, ushered to a separate room as though our presence might be disruptive or contagious.

Whenever I saw the opportunity to serve others, I met resistance. How could someone with cerebral palsy lead a Sunday school class? How would guests feel if greeted by someone in a wheelchair? The sentiment rose repeatedly even if the words were never spoken: "Stay in your corner. You're getting in the way of ministry." On the rare occasions I was given an opportunity to serve, the physical actions I was assigned, like painting a pillar, took me twice as long as the others. And in the pillar instance, after I had finished and had expended all my energy, someone came up behind me and repainted it!

Over time these tensions grew. I did not fit in anywhere. I felt trapped between the "disability world" and the "regular world." I was not disabled enough to fit into the "disability world" and not able-bodied enough to participate in the "regular world." At times, the tension threatened to tear me apart. I felt utterly worthless. How could anyone love me if I couldn't even paint a pillar? How could God love me?

I wondered if I could ever be a contributor in God's kingdom. For nineteen years, this fear grew. Even today, the tension lingers. This is one of the reasons I am so encouraged by your jumping into this book with us! Knowing you are reading this work and considering implementing our suggestions has given me a fresh outlook on ministry and life itself. The turnaround for me came when I formulated the Five-Step Plan, and a few select friends engaged with it. We hope you, too, will see the issues in our churches, commit yourself to the solution, and take up the baton. Run and roll with us.

THE HANDLER: DISTRACTED

When I (Paul) was growing up, my grade-school teachers accused me of not paying attention in class. I always chalked this up to their delivering long, uninteresting presentations. But deep down, I knew they were right. I was always in an impulsive rush. Math assignments were returned with the grader's comments in red, "Double-check your work!"

I interrupted conversations with others. I began projects but failed to complete them. I always misplaced or lost important items. In those days there were no clinical diagnoses for those of us labeled *scatterbrained* or *dreamers*. I used the mounting pressure of an approaching assignment deadline to force myself to complete a term paper or research project— never the best strategy for academic achievement.

I stumbled along with average grades until entering graduate school. I dreaded studying Greek and Hebrew, requirements for my master of theology degree. I knew seminary work was difficult; I'd heard the horror stories of students dropping out because of the unrelenting pace of biblical language acquisition, the intricate study of systematic theology, and the stress of producing interesting, accurate sermons. Seminary study is not for the faint of heart.

Finally, after years of consideration, I scheduled an appointment with a medical doctor. After a series of tests and interviews, my diagnosis was returned: ADHD non-hyperactive. I felt a sense of relief but also a feeling of shame. The label "attention deficit disorder" often carries negative connotations: stupid, airhead, ditzy, or lazy. The patron saint of ADD was Dory from the movie *Finding Nemo*. Of course, Dory is cute and lovable, but everyone laughs at her. Everyone knows she's not normal.[1] I was glad to get some relief through medication that a doctor prescribed. It helped me focus and stay on the task. Unfortunately, it also kept me awake at night and exhausted the next day.

All of this brings me to meeting my coauthor, Jason Epps. Internally, I related to persons with a disability. We each had some impairment. In many cases, PWDs were struggling with getting through the normal, everyday struggles of life just like me. I assumed they also wrestled with fitting in with others and discovering how they could best function on a team.

Now, before you write me off as whining about suffering from an insignificant disability, know that everyone with a disability feels the struggle and the shame of living with the Dory label: not normal. Disability experts describe this negative emotion as feeling *other than*. People with disabilities face isolation, loneliness, and less social support than those without disabilities.

So when one of my students, Jason Epps, wheeled into my homiletics classroom in his power chair, I felt both excitement and fear. How would he fit into our preaching class? After making it in through the heavy door, he saw the built-in, raised stage at the front of the classroom with no ramp. On top of that, I noticed the pulpit was a foot over his head in his seated position. The classroom was designed with little regard for students with disabilities.

---

1.   "Dory suffers from severe short-term memory loss, but a lot of what she goes through can be adapted to other contexts, such as the world, or ocean, of ADHD. Dory has trouble with multi-step directions, is easily distracted, and is very impulsive." James Poole, "Finding Dory: How It Relates to ADHD and What Parents Can Learn from the Fish," Fastbraiin, June 29, 2021, https://www.fastbraiin.com/blogs/blog/finding-dory-how-it-relates-to-adhd-and-what-parents-can-learn-from-the-fish.

But that one question Jason posed toward the end of our semester together led to this book: "Do you believe a church would hire me as their senior minister?" I knew better than to lie to Jason (and myself). Instead, I paused, took a deep breath, and muttered, "I don't know."

There are many pastors, priests, and religious leaders with disabilities of all types. At that moment, I was unaware and ill-informed. However, it is still a legitimate question now that I have also discovered there is quite a bit of discrimination directed toward full-time vocational ministry workers with disabilities.

At some point during each semester, I offer my students a deal. It goes like this: "I have written six books. If *I* can write a book, *you* can write a book. How many of you want to write a book or have an idea for a book you've been thinking about?" No one ever lifts their hand. Then I reframe the question, asking, "Look, I am not saying you *have* to write the book. I am simply asking how many of you *want* to write a book or have an *idea* for a book?" Slowly, hands begin inching up across the classroom. "Okay, the hardest part is getting started. If you will write the first chapter, I will read it, meet with you, and give you advice on what your next steps should be." Of the hundreds of students who have raised their hands, only two or three have ever taken me up on my offer.

Jason Epps was one of those students. This book is a result of my classroom gambit.

Part 1

DISABILITIES IN THE LOCAL CHURCH

Chapter 1

WHEN WE VISIT

A NEGATIVE NARROW DOOR

Trish maneuvered her wheelchair onto the front porch. Then she waited and waited.

She's late. Again. Her fingertips played with her pleated skirt. Floral. Knee-length. Flouncy. *I hope this is the right thing to wear. Lily said it's a casual church. Young. Not stiff.*

A car zipped down the road.

Not Lily. Trish sighed. *I mean. I get it. Why Lily left First Baptist. And Josh. And Evan. Eastside's younger. And they've got a young adults ministry that's perfect for us. I've thought about leaving. For a while. I've never fit in. Not really. Not fully. And there's nowhere for me to serve except as a prayer partner. Which is great. I'd just like to do something different for a change. But—I.* She looked at her watch. Then she ran her fingers through her hair. *It'd be easier to stay at First Baptist. So much easier. But I do miss my people. And, maybe, it won't be so difficult to switch. Or as difficult as I think it'll be. I just hope Eastside works since it's where they've all wound up going. Josh's already on the worship team. That's committed. And Lily really likes her new community group.* Trish peeked at her watch a second time. *I don't mind. Her being late. Really. It's just . . . what if it takes a long time to figure this new place out? The hallways? The elevators? What if we get there so late that people notice? Stare?* Her fingers drummed a rhythm on her armrest. *She was supposed to be here at ten-fifteen.* Trish pursed and released her lips several times. Pop. Pop. Pop. Waiting.

It was just . . . a lot.

A silver minivan pulled into the driveway like a bullet. Lily honked. The driver's door opened, and Lily—tripping on unstrapped sandals— narrowly avoided tumbling onto the gravel. "So sorry!"

"It's okay." Trish tossed her hand as if she did not mind. *I wish I didn't have to care. I wish it didn't matter. That I could show up late and not care. Too much, anyway.*

Lily entered the garage and then emerged with Trish's ramp. "I may have overslept." She pinched her fingers to indicate a minuscule amount. "A tad." Then Lily smiled an I-am-really-sorry smile.

Lily guided Trish as she angled her chair into the van, then she secured the wheelchair to the van floor with Trish sitting on top of the chair.

"Alright. Let's do this thing," Lily said, then closed the sliding door.

Trish swallowed. *Committed now.*

They listened to the local Christian station on the way to church. Lily belted out the lyrics. Trish sang along but with less gusto. Lily was a great friend. She had known Trish before the car accident. They had gone to church together for years, since college, and they had been in the same small group that whole time, so the pickup protocol was familiar even if the destination was different. Lily always kept the middle seats out of her minivan just for Trish. They spent a lot of time together, at coffee shops and game nights. Trish looked at her friend. Lily bobbed her neck back and forth like a head-banging lizard, and Trish grinned. *She rocks the mom van. Loud music. No French fries crammed into the cupholders and left to petrify. A pretty good life for a minivan.*

"That's it!" Lily pointed out the passenger-side window. "Eastside." It was an apartment building turned workspace wedged in between two other old downtown buildings. "We're on the second floor. With all the windows," she smiled.

"Very cool." Trish leaned over to peer out her window. All the plants peeking through the large panes of glass looked inviting. "I'm sure that's nice with all that natural light." She stared at her Converses. *Second floor. Their website says, "Wheelchair accessible." But is it really?*

Lily helped Trish get her and her chair out of the minivan, and they headed across the crosswalk and down the sidewalk.

A greeter stepped outside the church and propped open the doors. *Double-wide. Brilliant.*

"Morning, Chris!" Lily called.

"Hey, Lil! It's good to see you." He gave her a side hug, then extended his hand to Trish. "Who's your friend?"

"This is Trish," Lily answered. "She's one of my college friends. She's checking out Eastside."

"Awesome. It's nice to meet you, Trish."

"Same. It's good to meet you too."

Chris smiled, then motioned with his hand. "I'll see y'all inside. You'll find the elevator directly to your left."

They found the elevator around the corner. Trish and Lily squeezed inside. It was a tiny elevator, and a little shaky, but still an elevator.

The door slid open, and Trish rolled off. *Second floor? Made it.*

People lined the walls and smiled as Trish and Lily slipped through the parting sea of churchgoers.

"This way!" Lily called. "We'll find the guys. They'll be thrilled you're here!"

Lily jaunted off toward the fellowship hall. A warm, nutty scent saturated the air while people in their thirties strolled along the landing, carrying white foam cups filled with coffee. A few little kids scrambled past, clutching donut holes.

Lily crossed the veranda a little too quickly.

"Hey, Lily!" Trish called. "Lily!" *She didn't hear.*

A swath of people separated them, and Trish wound up at the back of the pack.

Trish watched Lily bounce to the far side of the fellowship area. Her friend swiped a cup of coffee off the bar and then joined Evan and Josh, chatting on the far side of the room. Lily took a swig of coffee with one hand while her other hand waved wildly, inviting Trish to join them.

Trish hesitated. *It'll take forever to get over. To make it through all these people. And I don't know them. And, if I go over there, Lily will want to get my coffee, but she's already helped so much.*

Lily kept waving.

Better go. If I don't, that'll draw more attention. Trish rolled past the sputtering coffee makers then wove through the room abuzz with a dozen different conversations.

"Hey, Trish!" Josh wrapped an arm around her shoulders. "It's so good to see you."

Evan handed Trish a napkin with a couple donut holes. "How've you been?"

"It's good to see y'all, too," she smiled. "Thanks."

Lily handed her a coffee, and they all chatted for a while. Josh caught them up on his work situation, and Evan showed them pictures of his new puppy (a golden retriever) and the remains of his chewed futon.

A little bit normal. Known.

Lily was explaining her summer plans when Josh glanced at his watch, then snapped and pointed his fingers. "Gotta go. I'm on bass today. See y'all in there."

"See you." Trish smiled.

The other three lingered a little longer until the room began clearing out. Lily looked at Trish. "Ready?"

"Let's do it," she nodded.

The trio made their way across the veranda and down a long hallway. A door stood open on the left-hand side at the far end of the hall. Thick trim bordered the doorframe, tall but narrow.

Trish tensed her jaw: an involuntary response. *Really skinny.*

Evan sauntered through the doorframe, then Lily.

It'll work. I'll make it work . . . I hope.

Evan and Lily waited inside.

Trish lined up her powered wheelchair. *Attempt number one? A no-go. But you didn't hit the doorframe.* A clump of latecomers clustered in the hallway. *Attempt number two.* The right wheel scuffed the doorframe, and the tire caught on the molding. *Ugh.* Trish looked up. Light filtered into the sanctuary, small and cozy and filled with growing things. Josh, his bass strapped around his neck, stood at the front of the sanctuary, watching her. He smiled. The encouraging grin failed to mask his concern. Trish looked down at her sneakers, and her face turned red. *Are other people looking too? Breathe. Don't rush. That won't help. Take your time. Do it right. Just breathe.* She made it through the doorway, a small margin on either side.

"Awesome. Let's go sit over there." Evan pointed at the second row. "I want to introduce y'all to Mason and Shae. They're our community group leaders. Mine and Lily's. We meet at their house on Tuesday nights."

Evan took a step, but Lily yanked his sleeve and shook her head.

Trish scanned the seating situation. Wheelchair spaces only existed in the back row. A few extra chairs had been removed to create reserved spaces. The rows toward the front held the maximum number of chairs-to-aisle ratio.

"Oh. Wait. Never mind. Let's sit here." Evan plopped into a chair next to an empty space. "I'll introduce y'all later."

Lily sat on the other side of the empty space, and Trish backed her chair into her spot at the back of the sanctuary.

The service started, but Trish felt like a kid staring into a fishbowl—a world observed but not entered. Lots of people their age filled the seats, along with a few younger families and older saints. *People my age. But still, no one quite like me. Not yet anyway. I wonder if there'll ever be someone else like me. If I'll ever be a part of it? Life here?*

The pastor trailed through his sermon notes, exegeting parables on mustard seeds and leaven and doors. Trish's mind wandered. *Will anyone want to talk after the service? Anyone I don't know? Will Evan remember to introduce us to that couple? What if they invite me to their community group? I wonder if their house is accessible.* The pastor transitioned to his application points. *I wonder if it's better to slip out during the last song. Before it ends rather than waiting? It'd be distracting to the worship if I can't angle my way out of the door the first time. But what if I wait until after the service, and I don't make it out the first time? Slipping out seems better than all the attention. Or I could wait until everyone else leaves? Or mostly leaves.* She exhaled. *I get that salvation's got a skinny door. But why can't churches have wide doors?*

Why do we have such skinny doors?

A CHANGE IN PERSPECTIVE

We understand that readers approach the topic of disability and ministry from various perspectives. Some are highly supportive and are doing all they can to celebrate their friends and family members with disabilities in a loving, belonging community. Others are neutral and have not spent much time or energy around friends with disabilities. A few readers might be antagonistic. However, regardless of your approach, we hope you finish this book convinced that the Western church has a problem with this issue.

Well, you might argue, our churches have tons of problems: our children's ministry is consistently understaffed, the roof has been leaking since the Flood, and we've never had a youth pastor stay longer than two years. Is welcoming and including PWDs that big of a problem? How often does your church welcome a visitor with a disability? Is this a primary issue for churches today?

To many non-disabled individuals, disability is a rare occurrence. In grocery stores, parks, and schools, non-disabled people make up most of the population. How often do you see accessible parking spots filled by vehicles with the appropriate hangtag?

Some of the challenges with seeing the size of this population is its diversity. Some disabilities are categorized as *stable*, meaning they are relatively unchanging. These could be individuals born without sight or veterans who have been injured in armed conflict. Others are labeled *degenerative*, meaning the person's health is generally declining. Many of the individuals in this category are older adults. Some disabilities are physical like spastic diplegia. Others are cognitive, such as Huntington's disease. Others, like cerebral palsy, can include both conditions. An *intellectual* or *developmental disability* (also called IDD) includes chronic conditions caused by mental and/or physical impairments.

Despite many people's perception, the reality is that one in five Americans—more than fifty-six million—are impacted by a disability. Having a disability is *normal*. When churches tailor their services and building to the non-disabled (whether intentionally or not), they exclude a fifth of the American population. For comparison, around one in five Americans live in the Midwest. What if someone stood outside the church holding a sign that read, "We're not ready for Midwesterners"? Or worse,

"Midwesterners not welcome here!"? The sheer number of people with a disability demands the church consider inclusivity a primary issue.

Statistical Scope of Disabilities

The number of people with a disability differs based on how "disability" is defined by the data collectors. According to the Centers for Disease Control and Prevention (CDC), sixty-one million adults in the United States live with a disability.[2] This means that 26 percent (one in four) of adults in the United States have some type of disability. In contrast, the 2021 American Community Survey (ACS) by the US Census Bureau states that only 13.4 percent of the American population have a disability.[3]

Both CDC and ACS use the same categories for determining disabilities:

1. Visual (blind or has serious difficulty seeing even when wearing glasses)
2. Hearing (deaf or has serious difficulty hearing)
3. Cognitive (serious difficulty concentrating, remembering, or making decisions because of a physical, mental, or emotional condition)
4. Ambulatory (serious difficulty walking or climbing stairs)
5. Self-care (difficulty dressing or bathing)
6. Independent living (difficulty doing errands alone such as visiting a doctor's office because of a physical, mental, or emotional condition)[4]

So, what causes such a drastic difference? The ACS employs a conservative number of only those with a "severe disability." The numbers presented tend to include fewer individuals than the CDC, which includes less severe disabilities such as ambulatory difficulties in older adults.[5]

We opt for a middle estimate of one out of five. This is between the ACS and CDC figures, acknowledging that half of this group identify their disability as severe. Whether citing the CDC or the ACS, disability issues and the needs surrounding the community are massive.

2. "Prevalence of Disability and Disability Types by Urban-Rural County Classific-ation—United States, 2016," Centers for Disease Control and Prevention, last updated 2021, https://www.cdc.gov/ncbddd/disabilityandhealth/features/dis-ability-prevalence-rural-urban.html.
3. "Selected Social Characteristics in the United States," American Community Survey, United States Census Bureau, last updated 2021, https://data.census.gov/table?q=DP02.
4. "Disability and Health Data System (DHDS)," CDC.
5. "Disability and Health Data System (DHDS)," CDC.

Most pastors feel as though their churches are sufficiently accessible for those with disabilities. According to a 2019 Lifeway Research survey, 99 percent of pastors feel that someone with disabilities would feel welcome at their church. Of congregants, 97 percent agree.[6] Yet, "only 5 to 10 percent of the world's disabled are effectively reached with the gospel, making the disability community one of the largest unreached . . . people groups in the world."[7] Many pastors and congregants without disabilities cannot see the physical and social hindrances to welcoming everyone to church.

A plethora of options often greet Christians in the United States. They can choose local church membership based on the perfect mixture of denomination, liturgy, theological convictions, worship style, church government, and overall vibe. However, these choices are a privilege not afforded to many with disabilities. In contrast to the actual numerical need, only one in five churches has any level of ministry to those with disabilities.[8]

A HISTORY OF DISABILITY STUDIES

History of Disability in Europe and the Americas

Providing equitable access to PWDs has not always been a concern. While impairment has always been a part of the human experience, "disability" is a social category that traces back to eighteenth-century European culture.[9] Lennard Davis, Distinguished Professor of English at the University of Illinois at Chicago, notes, "Disability is not so much the lack of a sense or the presence of a physical or mental impairment as it is

---

6. Aaron Earls, "Churches Believe They Are Welcoming to Those with Disabilities," *Lifeway Research,* March 10, 2020, https://research.lifeway.com/2020/03/10/churches-believe-they-are-welcoming-to-those-with-disabilities/.

7. "Lausanne Occasional Paper: Ministry Among People with Disabilities," Lausanne Movement, September 24, 2021, https://lausanne.org/content/ministry-among-people-disabilities-lop-35b.

8. Sarah Eekhoff Zylstra, "Let No Special Need Hinder the Spread of the Gospel," *The Gospel Coalition,* September 2, 2014, https://www.thegospelcoalition.org/article/let-no-special-need-hinder-the-spread-of-the-gospel/.

9. David L. Braddock and Susan L. Parish, "An Institutional History of Disability," in *Handbook of Disability Studies,* eds. Gary L. Albrecht, Katherine Delores Seelman, and Michael Bury (Thousand Oaks, CA: SAGE Publications, 2001), 13.

the reception and construction of that difference. . . . An impairment is a physical fact, but a disability is a social construction. For example, lack of mobility is an impairment, but an environment without ramps turns that impairment into a disability."[10]

For example, before the eighteenth century, a family's grandmother may have had limited mobility. Like today, her impairment would have been recognized. However, in a preindustrial environment, she would have had a strong social network and a smaller physical community who could adapt to her impairment. Grandma would not have been considered "disabled" just as much as children were not considered "disabled," although they both would have physical limits compared with young adults. However, the increasing industrialization and rigid urban environments transformed Grandma's impairment into a social category. She now belonged to a class of people who could not use stairs or stand at the power loom for hours on end. Impairments became hindrances to a productive society; they became "disabilities."[11]

Despite the lack of terminology, PWDs have always faced harsh realities. In pre-Christian Greek and Roman society, popular culture viewed those born with visible disabilities as bearing divine wrath and were summarily put to death. According to Spartan law, babies born with physical deformities were to be killed, even if the family were wealthy and could afford to raise their child with appropriate care.[12] This stigma, however, did not carry over to adults with disabilities.[13] The lack of medical care and danger of most professions made disability and deformity normative for many adults during this time.[14] Many people who became disabled later in life (such as those injured in war) remained in society. A physical disability from battle, however, did not exclude a soldier from carrying on in his profession; whether he walked or limped, he readied for battle.

---

10. Lennard J. Davis, *Enforcing Normalcy: Disability, Deafness, and the Body* (Brooklyn, NY: Verso, 1995), 56.
11. Braddock and Parish, "An Institutional History of Disability," 13.
12. Braddock and Parish, "An Institutional History of Disability," 15.
13. Braddock and Parish, "An Institutional History of Disability," 13.
14. Braddock and Parish, "An Institutional History of Disability," 15.

In the Christian Middle Ages, the response varied. Between the fourth and sixth centuries CE, Christians built and maintained support facilities for those with impaired vision in Turkey, Syria, and France. In the thirteenth century, Christians in Geel, Belgium, began a family care facility for those experiencing a mental disability.[15] The poor and disenfranchised (often people with disabilities) held a unique place in the social context of Christian Europe. In the Rule of Saint Benedict, the needy were closer to Christ by merit of their poverty and gave the better-off an opportunity to express hospitality as a means of serving Christ.[16]

However, as superstition and fear of satanic possession rose—stirred on by plagues which ravaged Europe—PWDs (especially those with seizure disorders) faced violence and accusations. While persecution was real, it was limited to certain cities at certain times. Most medical texts on maladies, including seizures, provided herbal or therapeutic remedies rather than spiritual intervention. The social and moral expectation for villages was to care for people with disabilities in their community.[17]

After the Middle Ages, the Enlightenment and explosion of scientific categories led to more effective treatment for sickness and impairments. However, they also began to normalize non-disability in Western culture, viewing those with impairments as deviants. "Normal" people had no disabilities. The Enlightenment led to the Industrial Revolution, which solidified "disabled" as a nonnormative social category.[18]

The development of mental health facilities in the West (beginning in the nineteenth century) started off well. However, prisons soon began sending their more difficult inmates. Communities were eager to send problematic individuals to the facilities. This led to severe overcrowding, pessimism about social reintegration, and poor care.[19] In the early twentieth century, the view that PWDs were genetically inferior led to discrimination, segregation, and violence. The influence of Darwinism

---

15. Braddock and Parish, "An Institutional History of Disability," 17.
16. Irina Metzler, *A Social History of Disability in the Middle Ages: Cultural Considerations of Physical Impairment* (London: Taylor & Francis Group, 2013), 156.
17. Braddock and Parish, "An Institutional History of Disability," 18.
18. Braddock and Parish, "An Institutional History of Disability," 13.
19. Braddock and Parish, "An Institutional History of Disability," 33.

and the rise in eugenics led medical communities often to refuse to treat newborns with disabilities, letting them die so that they would not pass along their "inferior" genetics.[20] Forced sterilization of those with intellectual disabilities was common. In the 1927 Supreme Court decision *Buck v. Bell*, the government's right to sterilize those deemed "feebleminded" or "idiots" was approved.[21] The decision of *Buck v. Bell* has not been reversed at the time of this book's publication. Because PWDs rarely recorded their experiences, most historical data for disability is limited to professional and clinical records.[22]

In 2019, the US Department of Justice published a report which states those with disabilities are four times more likely to be victims of violent crimes compared with their non-disabled counterparts. Since 2009, the percentage of victimizations has been on the rise, with simple assaults (minor injuries), robberies, aggravated assaults (serious injuries or weapons present), and sexual assaults all rising.[23]

However, beginning in the West in the 1940s, PWDs began to speak about their experiences. This revolutionized how culture perceived disability, and new models of disability grew from this new perception. As stories and social awareness grew, those with similar disabilities shared their experiences and fought for equity.[24]

History of Disability in Asia and Africa

Eastern cultures from the time of Christ onward have had a unique take on understanding PWDs. We will look at the Ottoman Empire, Kenya, and China as representative cultures, but these do not summarize the whole of an Eastern perspective.

The word "disabled" does not appear in Arabic until the twentieth century, which aligns with the word's appearance a few decades prior in Europe. Ottoman culture had an awareness of impairments, but the

---

20. Braddock and Parish, "An Institutional History of Disability," 38.
21. Braddock and Parish, "An Institutional History of Disability," 40.
22. Braddock and Parish, "An Institutional History of Disability," 12.
23. Erika Harrell, "Crime Against Persons with Disabilities, 2009–2019 – Statistical Tables," US Department of Justice, November 4, 2021, https://bjs.ojp.gov/library/publications/crime-against-persons-disabilities-2009-2019-statistical-tables.
24. Braddock and Parish, "An Institutional History of Disability," 13.

social category of disability is new in both the East and the West.[25] The nearest correlation to people with disabilities was "people with defects," to denote nonnormative physical features, such as phocomelia, warts, and even blue eyes in non-medical literature.[26] The lack of social category did not protect those with impairments from discrimination and social isolation. Violence and inability to find work often hindered those with impairments.

However, the story is not all negative. During the Ottoman rule between the sixteenth and nineteenth centuries, many voluntary societies aimed to support PWDs financially and socially.[27] Religious charity and the requirement of family care helped protect against discrimination and abuse.[28]

Religious sentiment in Kenya often drove popular attitudes toward people with disabilities. If a priest or religious leader believed that a child was born cursed or that God was upset with someone who experienced disability later in life, communities would agree. Some perceived that PWDs could not contribute to their community, which led to social isolation and the perception of "worthlessness."[29] At the end of the twentieth century, Christian faith healers were common, and those who could not be healed were often condemned for their lack of faith.[30]

Prior to the twenty-first century, those with disabilities in China were often termed *fei ren*, which means "garbage people."[31] People with disabilities—especially severe or visible disabilities—were physically and socially ostracized. Then Deng Pufang impacted modern Chinese policy. Deng Pufang was crippled at the waist after interactions with the Red Guard during Maoist governance in China. The details of whether

25. Sara Scalenghe, *Disability in the Ottoman Arab World, 1500–1800*, Cambridge Studies in Islamic Civilization (New York: Cambridge University Press, 2014), 1.

26. Scalenghe, *Disability in the Ottoman Arab World*, 2.

27. Scalenghe, *Disability in the Ottoman Arab World*, 12.

28. Scalenghe, *Disability in the Ottoman Arab World*, 82.

29. Samuel Kabue, *Disability, Society, and Theology: Voices from Africa* (Limuru, Kenya: Zapf Chancery Publishers Africa, 2011), 111.

30. Kabue, *Disability, Society, and Theology*, 113–114.

31. Matthew Kohrman, *Bodies of Difference: Experiences of Disability and Institutional Advocacy in the Making of Modern China* (Berkeley: University of California Press, 2005), 31.

Deng Pufang was imprisoned, beaten, or attempted suicide is uncertain, but after falling three stories from a window, Deng Pufang lost function of his legs.[32] Deng Pufang's father, Deng Xiaoping, rose to power and implemented reforms after Mao Zedong's death. Encouraged by his son, Deng Xiaoping created the China Disabled Persons' Federation, which worked to improve the position of people with disabilities in China.[33] The current term for those with a disability is *canji ren*, which means "disabled people." Awareness of PWDs and a push for person-first language is growing in modern China.[34]

DISABILITY STUDIES TODAY

Two models of disability have profoundly impacted disability studies today. The *social model* argues the essence of "disability" is not impairment, but rigid social and physical environments which hinder full participation. Thus, for someone with a visual impairment, their impairment is not the *primary* issue, but rather the perception they are nonnormative and, thus, social outliers. In this view, those with a disability often suffer more from their inaccessible environment than from the impairment itself.

The 1970s brought the *independent living and self-advocacy model*, which carried an emphasis on non-institutionalization and appropriate independence. If disability is not only an impairment, but a social—and often restrictive—category, when PWDs can live in communities where they express self-advocacy and appropriate independence, they can thrive.[35]

Our own viewpoint aligns with both models. Just as individuals with disabilities should not be shuffled off into institutions apart from society, they should not be separated from the church community into special classes. Additionally, people with disabilities cannot be seen as social "others," but as productive and essential members of the faith community.

---

32. Kohrman, *Bodies of Difference*, 33.
33. Kohrman, *Bodies of Difference*, 32.
34. Kevin Avery, "Disability and the Three Traditional Chinese Belief Systems," *China Source Quarterly*, March 7, 2016, https://www.chinasource.org/resource-library/articles/disability-and-the-three-traditional-chinese-belief-systems/.
35. Braddock and Parish, "An Institutional History of Disability," 48.

A Note About Context

While we desire to have a global perspective, we must confess that we speak from our Western perspective. Nearly 80 percent of the global population with disabilities live in the Global South. Yet most modern scholarship and global relief initiatives rely on Western practices and assumptions.[36] Helen Meekosha writes, "Contemporary disability studies constitutes a form of scholarship colonialism."[37] While the emphasis in Western disabilities studies is integration and belonging, the focus in many non-Western contexts is prevention and medical intervention.[38]

As such, we urge churches to remain open-minded when interacting with those from other cultural contexts. Especially for churches in the West who hope to minister to those outside the Western context—such as immigrants, refugees, and international students—humility and willingness to listen are paramount.

36. Scalenghe, *Disability in the Ottoman Arab World*, 8.
37. Helen Meekosha, "Decolonising Disability: Thinking and Acting Globally," *Disability & Society* 26, no. 6 (September 2011): 668.
38. Scalenghe, *Disability in the Ottoman Arab World*, 9.

A Place in the Body: Kasey's Story

My husband and I felt it in our hearts to adopt a child who otherwise would not find a home and a family. As we explored, we found that children with special needs rarely find families willing to care for them. We started the process for a special-needs adoption.

Our church was supportive. They helped us financially with the process. However, the first time I shared with a group of women that we would be adopting a child with special needs, I was met with awkward silence—and then praise about how noble of a cause this was to them. On the inside I didn't feel noble; I felt terrified. I remember crying the first time we met the boy who would be our son. I cried because I was afraid and heartbroken by his suffering. To those women who thought I was a noble saint, how could I share that I was terrified?

We brought our son home in January of 2017. He had global delays and required intensive therapy. Our first few months were packed with doctor and therapy appointments.

At church, we started off taking him to the nursery. Soon, the children's ministry volunteers began finding me during the first few minutes of worship. They needed my help. But I didn't have all the answers. I was learning, too. I felt self-conscious about my own lack of knowledge and experience and overwhelmed that I not only needed to figure out how to be a caregiver to a special needs toddler but also was being asked to train others as well. We were barely keeping our heads above water.

It was soon clear that our church could not learn to care for our son. My husband and I took turns going to church for a long time. He would go one Sunday, and I would stay home with our son. We switched every Sunday. Church was an important part of our life and relationship with God. Neither of us wanted to lose that.

The summer after our adoption was complete, I joined a women's Bible study at our church. The study taught about what it meant to be a "godly woman." One lesson revolved around the responsibility to promote a peaceful home. My home wasn't peaceful. My home had a child who would scream for 2–4 hours a day at the top of his lungs, needed breathing treatments around the clock, and could not eat without constant safety supervision. My home was not peaceful. Was I not a godly woman? I was living this reality *because* I had been obedient to God in the adoption.

One day I found out about a church that took care of children with special needs. I emailed the director of the program and explained in detail the wide range of our three-year-old son's needs. I finished the email pleading, "Would you be able to take care of him so we can go to church together?"

I held my breath.

"Yes, no problem. When do you want to come?"

I was blown away at the simplicity of that email. My husband and I decided to go to church there for a few weeks to rest. I asked them if we could just come for a few weeks while we refueled. We were told to come for as long as we would like. Our "refuel" ended up being a permanent move. We joined the church just a couple of months later. Our son is now 8, and the church is still home to us.

I learned that people with special needs should be *more* than cared for by the church. They should also be celebrated, served, and desired as a necessary part of the body of Christ. Our son was celebrated. He received quality care. We as parents were given a respite. We were given channels for support, prayer, and shared wisdom from other parents in similar situations. Our entire family was treated as members of the spiritual community.

God uses all people and desires to have a relationship with all kinds of people. Ability level isn't a factor. This truth was lived out at Irving Bible Church in Irving, Texas.

———————

The church stands at the edge of a powerful shift. Our response to PWDs can change families and revolutionize communities. While those with disabilities seem to be an invisible population, they compose nearly one-fifth of the United States population.

A lack of physical and social accessibility hurts churches. Lamar Hardwick, the lead pastor at Tri-Cities Church in East Point, Georgia, and self-described "autism pastor," writes, "Families impacted by autism are nearly 84 percent more likely to never attend religious services due to a felt lack of inclusion."[39] Not only that, but "46 percent of families impacted by disability have never been asked how their child and family could be included in the life of the church."[40] Too many churches are comfortable with few to no individuals with a disability in their congregations.

We hope experiencing a church from the perspective of someone with a disability, the data, and a historical perspective has convinced you the church must reconsider and engage with this critical community. Historically, stories and voices of those facing discrimination have stirred social change. Throughout this book, we will share our own stories of disability and stories from others. We pray realizing these challenges will spark a revolution in your local faith community.

In the next two chapters, we reveal hidden barriers to full integration. Consider your own church and ministry. Are you unintentionally telling more than fifty-six million people they are not welcome? How narrow are your doors? How wide is your gospel message?

---

39. Lamar Hardwick, *Disability and the Church: A Vision for Diversity and Inclusion* (Downers Grove, IL: IVP, 2021), 18.
40. Hardwick, *Disability and the Church*, 18.

Chapter 2

PHYSICAL BARRIERS

FACILITIES FOR ALL

Actions speak louder than words, but money uses a megaphone. On average, American churches spend around 23 percent of their annual budget on facilities.[1] Congregations allocate these funds toward things like appliance repair, cleaning, and rent. Lots of churches view creating and maintaining a physical space as a critical part of God-honoring stewardship, but what type of building are they maintaining? Does the space reflect God's heart for his people?

Many find it tempting to consider accessible-architecture features as helpful additions—add-ons provided for convenience's sake. Often, churches have designed their buildings for non-disabled people. Accessible-architecture features or extras are viewed as helpful to the congregation, not as supports that foster the ability of people with disabilities to become more fully integrated into the regular rhythm of the body of

---

1. The National Study of Congregations' Economic Practices, Lake Institute on Faith & Giving, 2019, https://www.nscep.org/finding/.

Christ. Churches often view accessible elevators, parking spaces, and doorways as changes to the normal building rather than part of the building project itself. From that viewpoint, a ramp to the stage or podium is nonnormative, a not-necessarily-necessary extra in addition to the necessary stairs. However, we believe *the normative church building should be accessible.* A church without ramps, railings, and wheelchair-accessible doorways is not a "normal" church.

Imagine you are a parent visiting a new church. You walk into the children's ministry wing to find beige walls and a mauve carpet. Nobody greets you or tells you where to check in or about the check-in process. In fact, there is nowhere to check in your child. You take your toddler to the first room and peek inside. Somebody stuffed adult-sized chairs around a table, and a PowerPoint title slide, "The Historical Geography of Israel," flickers on the wall. A coffee station sits in the corner. Adult scissors lay on the floor, a sharp object left behind by the quilting group. No toys. No music. No Goldfish. You find a volunteer, sitting in the corner and thumbing through a pamphlet, and you ask them, "Where is the children's ministry?"

They respond, "Right here!"

If you were that parent, we hope you would turn right around. Without secure check-in procedures, an appropriate curriculum, and at least one plastic Noah's Ark (with a missing rhinoceros), the room fails to function as a children's ministry classroom. A space's purpose determines that space's facilities (form follows function), not the other way around. If a space serves as a space for children, that space's facilities are designed, chosen, and installed with those children in mind. In the same way, the purpose of the church is to be a "house of prayer" for all God's people—people with and without disabilities. The purpose should determine the facility; the facility should not determine the purpose.

What about churches with older buildings? So many of our church buildings were completed well before the implementation of the Americans with Disabilities Act of 1990. Those churches have served as gifts to God's people, enabling them to meet in an already finished and usually furnished structure, but older churches filled with narrow flights of stairs and multiple landings were not designed to be a place of worship with all of God's people in mind. Many churches have inherited buildings built for non-disabled people. What are some of the physical barriers to an inclusive church? Below, we document some of the common problem areas in churches. Think of them like leaky roofs, malfunctioning AC units, or perpetually flushing toilets. Technically, the service can still go on, but everyone knows there is a problem!

Boots on the Ground: Darryl's Story

I'm fifty-one years old, and I've been a member of my church since I was twelve. I remained involved in our youth group until I graduated and moved out of town. I came and went from that church for about ten years, but the church always accepted me as family when I visited. I returned to that church for good when I entered my late twenties. I established a good life for my three children and myself. I had an excellent job and obtained a new car and a new home approval. Then at thirty years old, on my way to a preapproved home interview on January 21, 2002, I was paralyzed in a car accident.

I spent two months in the hospital and then rehab. During that time, my church built a wheelchair-accessible room for me in my parents' garage. Since the accident, my church has always made front-row seating space available for me, and my name is on a wheelchair-accessible parking space. Some home builders in my church offered me a huge discount and built me a wheelchair-accessible home.

Other church members have completed a number of repairs to my home and even purchased new appliances for me. My pastor also purchased my van, and then I equipped it with hand controls, swivel seating, and a lift. My church has always been a huge part of my life and supported me throughout my life, no matter what that looks like.

ADA FOR THE CHURCH

Overview

In 1988, the Americans with Disabilities Act (ADA) was introduced to the US Congress. On July 26, 1990, the act was signed at the White House. The main champion for this legislation was Kansas senator Robert

Dole, who was severely injured in World War II. The ADA was a grass-roots movement of individuals, advocates, and organizations who wanted everyone to be treated equally—regardless of ability. The ADA comprises five titles. Title III describes the accessibility requirements for businesses and nonprofits (except for religious organizations) that are open to the public. Our discussion will focus on Title III.

The ADA strives to protect PWDs from discrimination. American businesses cannot construct their buildings in ways that restrict access to customers based on their disability status. While businesses must provide accessible buildings, religious organizations remain exempt from following ADA protocol.

So, can churches ignore the ADA? Yes and no. Legally, religious enti-ties are exempt from complying with the ADA. However, we are convinced our church facilities and fellowships should be more welcoming than a local restaurant. If our preachers affirm from their pulpits that everyone is welcome to hear the gospel, then why are so few church facilities or seminary classrooms measuring up to basic federal compliance?

We do not mean to oversimplify the issue. Many churches and Christian colleges have inherited buildings constructed for those without disabilities. Finances play a role in deciding how to revise facilities, and finances are not usually readily available. Yet, for most congregations, ADA compliance is easy to attain and provides the minimum of accessi-bility for those in the disability ministry. A convenient way for churches to move toward ADA-compatibility is for churches to replace equipment with accessible parts once they break. Doing so also opens the space to nonreligious renters (like the local government using the building for polling) who are obligated to comply with the ADA.

Our hope is that most church leaders are unaware of the ADA's re-quirements, that those regulations have slipped their notice or remained a vague acronym. For those looking to begin the process of church accessi-bility, this section aims to break down the ADA into accessible language.

Parking

Parking continues to be one of the largest challenges that either keeps or fails to keep members of a local assembly safe. However, we have good news. Transforming your church's parking lot into an ADA-compliant parking lot only requires three ingredients: a few cans of pavement paint, a pinch of time, and a dash of ingenuity.

Drop-off zones are areas (ideally under an awning, in case of rain) where someone who needs assistance can exit their vehicle safely. Currently, many drop-off zones are uncovered or in a high-traffic section of the parking lot. Creating a specific, orderly, and safe space for passenger drop-off will decrease a major hurdle to physical accessibility. This zone can function for various individuals with mobility issues: a veteran in her powered wheelchair, a child who uses forearm crutches, an older congregant with bad knees, and a teenager who recently sprained his ankle. Depending on the size of your congregation, the drop-off zone can be multipurpose.

Per the ADA, businesses must provide accessible parking spots with easy access to the facility. To be accessible, a parking spot must be eight feet wide; however, every sixth spot must be van-accessible, which means those parking spots must be eleven feet wide. All spots (whether regular or van-accessible) must have a five-foot wide access aisle next to it running the length of the parking spot on either side. This means one parking spot must have two access lanes; however, those lanes can be shared with another accessible spot if the parking is not angled. For angled parking, the access aisle must be on the passenger side. If you have seen a rectangle with diagonal lines next to a parking spot, those are access aisles.

The pavement around the parking spot must be stable, solid, and slip resistant. The parking spot may have a slight incline, but the incline must be no more than a 1.48 (2.08%) slope in all directions. Spots must be marked with the international symbol of accessibility at least five feet from the ground. Van-accessible spots must have an additional sign.

The number of accessible parking spaces depends on the overall number of parking spots. If the total number of overall parking spots is four or less, businesses must only have one accessible parking spot, but it must be van-accessible (eleven feet wide with an access aisle on both sides). However, the spot does not need to be marked with signage. The chart below from the ADA website shows the minimum number of required accessible parking spaces based on number of overall parking spots.

Guidelines for ADA-Compliant Parking Spaces	
Total Number of Parking Spaces Provided in Parking Facility	**Minimum Number of Required Accessible Parking Spaces**
1 to 25	1
26 to 50	2
51 to 75	3
76 to 100	4
101 to 150	5
151 to 200	6
201 to 300	7
301 to 400	8
401 to 500	9
501 to 1000	2 percent of total
1001 and over	20, plus 1 for each 100, or fraction thereof, over 1000

Advice from an Asset: Provide loading zones and parking spaces for people who utilize wheelchairs, then *maintain* them. Ensure the congregation respects those who utilize those zones and spaces by clearly designating and enforcing appropriate usage.

1. Provide a loading area for wheelchairs at least three feet wide if the ADA's five-foot access aisle is not possible.
2. Post signs to designate certain spaces as wheelchair parking only.
3. Provide separate parking spaces for those with mobility disabilities, including veterans.

Consider marking the pathway to the ramp in the sidewalk, clearly designating the ideal path when the accessible parking spots are far from the ramp or other accessible point of entry. In addition, clearly mark the edge with paint or textured surface, especially if the makeshift ramp is old or difficult to spot especially when it is dark.

Adequate Parking: Ryan's Story

Our current church campus does not provide adequate parking. It makes it exceedingly difficult for me to load and unload my son safely when the parking situation requires that I pull out into a parking lot filled with lots of traffic. I emailed someone regarding this issue, and recently the new campus pastor tried to assist me with parking. We were both treated with hostility by our fellow churchgoers.

Entrances and Doorways

Most entrances and doorways to church sanctuaries or auditoriums are already ADA-compliant. The ADA only requires that one entrance be accessible, but churches should check that their accessible entrance is close to accessible parking. If some entrances are accessible and others are inaccessible, the accessible entrances should be marked with signage.

What makes an entrance accessible? First, the doorway must be at least thirty-two inches wide, but thirty-six inches or more is preferable. The doorway cannot have any steps or landings, as they cannot be easily traversed by individuals with limited mobility. Doorways can be accessible even if they do not have a push-to-open activation switch or handicap push plate. However, during the times that the building is open (such as before, during, and after a worship service), someone must be standing at the doors to open them, or they must be propped open.

Ensure that the doorknobs of interior doors are accessible to those with arthritis or a weak grip. Round doorknobs should be replaced by lever handles. Replacing doorknobs serves as an inexpensive way to make a space accessible. All of this advice also pertains to Christian graduate schools and seminaries. Those who oversee local Christian schools, nonprofits, and parachurch organizations should always check with local authorities regarding ADA compliance. This is not only the right thing to do but provides a welcome witness to the watching community.

Advice from an Asset: Many churches shuffle their accessible parking, drop-off zones, and entrances away from the main entrance. For many individuals, however, this creates a silo effect. Those with mobility issues are ushered into the corner with a "special" entrance. Many main entrances are "non-disabled entrances." If everyone belongs at church, the main entrance must be accessible to everyone.

While technically the ADA only requires one entrance to be accessible, consider making as many as possible accessible, or ensuring the accessible entrance is not blocked. It is also helpful to clearly mark, via signs or other indicators, where the accessible entrance is located. In some cases, an entrance has been clearly marked as inaccessible but there is no clear indication as to how to get to the accessible entrance.

Stairwells

While it might be tempting to think the addition of an elevator addresses the ADA's accessibility requirements, the ADA also provides requirements regarding stairwells. Those requirements promote safety and accessibility for everyone who utilizes those spaces.

Firstly, the ADA's requirements stipulate the steps belonging to a stairwell must have uniform riser heights and uniform tread widths. The height and width of a step belonging to a particular stairwell must be uniform with all the other steps belonging to that stairwell. At a minimum, a step's tread must be no less than eleven inches wide, measured from the front riser to the back riser across the top of the step. The ADA does not permit open risers, stairs with gaps in between the treads or tops of the individual steps. The nosing or cap on the edge of each step must project no more than one and a half inches, otherwise the undersides of those nosings turn into tripping hazards. The leading edge of the tread should not be greater than one half inch. The underside of the nosing or cap must be sloped or cut at an angle that is not less than sixty degrees from the horizontal or flat top belonging to the individual step.

Handrails must run along both sides of the stairwell, and those handrails must meet the following specifications: They must be continuous along both sides of the stairwell. If the stairwell follows a switchback pattern, the inside handrail that runs along the switchback must also be continuous. If for some reason the handrails are not continuous, the handrails must have a horizontal extension (the bars that run horizontal, parallel to the floor) at the top and bottom of the run. The ADA requires a minimum twelve-inch horizontal extension at the top of each riser. The ADA also requires a minimum twelve-inch horizontal extension plus the width of one tread at the bottom of a particular flight of stairs.

Concerning handrails that are not continuous, the requirements also state that the handrails must continue at least twelve inches beyond the top riser found at the top of the stairwell and at least twelve inches plus the width of one tread beyond the bottom riser found at the bottom of the stairwell. At the top of the stairwell, that extension ought to run parallel with the floor while the extension at the bottom ought to continue to follow a slope for a distance the width of one tread out from the bottom riser with the rest of the extension that runs past that one-tread's–worth measurement being horizontal to the ground.

Additionally, the amount of open space that exists between the handrails and the wall ought to be an inch. Any gripping surfaces must be uninterrupted by newel posts or any other obstructions, including construction elements. The top of the handrail gripping surface must be mounted between thirty-four and thirty-eight inches above stair nosings. The ends of the handrails ought to be rounded or run smoothly until they return to the floor, wall, or post. Handrails must not rotate or slide around inside their fittings. The rails ought to be held securely in place. Stairs must have some kind of detectable warning alerting people to their presence, and outdoor stairs and the paths leading to those stairs need to be designed in such a way that water does not accumulate on walking surfaces. If these requirements sound tedious, imagine those with disabilities trying to navigate noncompliant buildings!

Advice from an Asset: The presence of the stairwell does not necessarily mean the area is inaccessible. However, some creative thinking might be required. For example, depending on the height of the stairwell, a simple ramp could suffice. There might also be an alternative entrance that is not obvious. Even if there is an elevator, the elevator might be too small or completely unreliable. Since different people have different views of whether a place is accessible, in-person observation is invaluable. For example, I (Jason) have been to several locations that were marked as handicapped accessible, but there was no accessible entrance. But I have also been on several trails that technically were not accessible according to ADA standards, but I was able to transverse them. It depends on the asset's individual limitations and the potential resources available to help. However, nothing is as valuable as a determined friend. I've had friends who have carried me and my manual chair up stairs that would put the pyramids to shame!

Bathrooms

While building codes emphasize the number and types of bathroom fixtures required by facilities, the ADA standards focus on which bathroom fixtures and features must be accessible when those fixtures and features are provided. While new building codes require all bathrooms, to provide access for everyone including employee bathrooms, provide access for everyone regardless of their disability status, in locations where single-room bathrooms are gathered at one place, at least half of those single-room bathrooms must comply with ADA standards. Regarding portable units, at least 5 percent of those portable units must comply with ADA standards, although portable units on construction sites remain fully exempt from those standards.

According to ADA requirements, single-room bathrooms compliant with accessibility standards must be clearly labeled as accessible by the International Symbol of Accessibility unless all single-room bathrooms are compliant in a particular area within that building space.

In facilities that provide multiuser bathrooms, unisex, single-use bathrooms cannot serve as a substitute for access to multiuser bathrooms unless the construction required to make the multiuser bathrooms accessible remains otherwise impossible. Multiuser and single-room bathrooms must comply with ADA standards. The provision of an accessible unisex bathroom in addition to the provision of multiuser bathrooms is helpful and shows consideration for people with disabilities whose personal care assistants are of the opposite sex. The International Building Code requires accessible unisex bathrooms in assembly and mercantile spaces that require a total of six or more toilet fixtures. The ADA standards require that unisex toilet rooms provide privacy latches and contain at minimum a lavatory, water closet, and urinal.

Lots of churches and schools inherit older buildings. While not required by law, many places of worship desire to comply with ADA standards. When alterations are made to already existing bathrooms, ADA standards only apply to the bathroom that undergoes the alterations. If one bathroom in an older church building receives any kind of update, that bathroom needs to be brought up to the ADA standards. The rest of the bathrooms in that same church building do not necessarily need to be brought up to those standards if no updates are made. The requirement to bring things up to ADA standards in the bathrooms receiving updates only applies to the features in a bathroom that receive the updates. For example, if grab bars in a bathroom receive an update, the new grab bars must be brought up to standard, but if the faucet controls remain unaltered, those faucet controls do not need to be brought up to standard.

Alterations are not required when those alterations fail to be technically feasible. Even so, it is within the best interests of all the people in the body of Christ to bring all features, or as many features as possible, up to ADA standards. Technical feasibility relates to a structure's capacity to change regarding things like adjustments to load-bearing walls. When it is not an option for an already existing multiuse bathroom to follow the standards, an accessible unisex bathroom located on the same floor as the multiuse bathroom should meet ADA requirements. An accessible path for travel to the bathrooms is also required. That path must extend from the entrance or arrival point to the bathrooms.

Regarding water closets, standards apply to the toilet's location, clearance, seating, grab bars, flush controls, and dispensers. To meet ADA standards, water closets require enough clearance space for PWDs to approach and transfer to the water closet as needed. Bathroom fixtures (aside from grab bars, toilet paper dispensers, seat covers, coat hooks, shelves, and sanitary napkin disposal units) must not encroach on the water closet's clearance space. The toilet's flush controls must be on the open side, not between the toilet and the nearest wall, and the seat ought to be seventeen to nineteen inches above the floor.

The standard requires mounting grab bars on the walls beside and behind the water closet. Grab bars can be separate or continuous. The bars along with the walls surrounding the bars must remain free of any abrasive or sharp objects. Any projecting features such as shelves or disposal units must be located at least twelve inches above the grab bars or one and a half inches from the bottom and ends of the grab bars so as not to impact the usage of the grab bars. All bars must possess rounded edges. The space between the grab bar and the wall, a one-and-a-half-inch clearance, prevents people from getting entrapped by the bar.

Grab bars must be capable of bearing a vertical or horizontal force of 250 pounds at any point along the grab bar along with any fasteners, mounting devices, and support structures associated with the bar. If folding or swing-away grab bars are provided, those bars must be secure, and they must not interfere with the usage of the required grab bars or the clearance space surrounding the water closet. Toilet paper dispensers must be placed within easy reach of the water closet either below or above the grab bars.

Concerning doors and enough turning space, no bathroom features can overlap the full range of the door's opening and closing clearance since all that space may be required for people utilizing mobility aids to enter the room and clear the door. Sufficient interior turning space must also be provided, a minimum of a sixty-inch diameter circle or a T-shaped space anywhere inside the bathroom. Doors may swing into the turning space. Bathroom fixtures may also overlap that turning space, but those fixtures must allow for toe and knee clearance. Baby changing tables must be placed in such a way that a forward approach is possible.

Inside multiuse bathrooms, at least one compartment must be wheelchair accessible. That compartment must be outfitted with doors offset from the water closet so that there is enough space for a wheelchair to enter the compartment. The doors may be hinged to the left or right side of the compartment, but those doors must include a minimum clearance of thirty-two inches and the appropriate hardware as well as withstand a maximum opening force of five pounds. Requirements related to single-use restrooms apply to wheelchair-accessible compartments. Wheelchair-accessible compartments built at the end of a row allow for those compartments to utilize more empty space, allowing for a larger and more maneuverable compartment.

If a lavatory is included in the compartment, that compartment must meet the space requirements for a water closet or single-use restroom rather than the minimum amount of space for the single-use compartment. Ambulatory-accessible compartments accommodate people who use walking devices such as canes or crutches by lining both sides of the compartment with grab bars. Ambulatory compartments are not built for wheelchair accessibility and must be provided in bathrooms with six or more compartments or a combined total of six compartments and urinals. If two or more urinals are present in a bathroom, at least one urinal must comply.

Advice from an Asset: First and foremost, just because a stall is marked as handicap accessible does not mean there is necessarily enough space for the person with a disability. Especially in places like airports, the handicap stall is barely wider than the standard stall. In addition, the ADA does not require automatic door openers in bathrooms. One of the tricky situations is physically being able to exit the room since it is often easier to find someone on the outside willing to open the door for you to enter. Therefore, in some cases the handler might need to stay outside the restroom to ensure the asset is not trapped.

When the handler is doing an additional survey and research of a location (which we'll talk about in part 3), it is always helpful to keep an eye out for companion bathrooms, not only because of the extra space they provide, but also for the flexibility if the asset has a personal care attendant. As awkward as the conversation might be, it would be helpful to discuss with the asset what their needs might be as it pertains to using the facilities. It is always best if expectations are clearly established between the two.

Ideally, the handler should not feel obligated to go further than what they feel comfortable with. Discussing these situations prior to need not only allows for clearer communication, but also for better input. For instance, the assets may require grab bars, or they may not. Space may be a greater concern to them because of their wheelchair or other adaptive aids. This subject is one of the most sensitive and should always be tailored to the individual.

BEYOND ADA

The ADA standards do not cover some of the everyday aspects found in most churches. Accessibility to the stage, the baptismal or the communion rail, and the coffee bar are some of the spaces common throughout our churches, and accessibility to those spaces and spaces like them ought to be normative for our churches.

Stage

For all the members within the body of Christ to participate in the church service, especially in leadership or worship roles, it is imperative that the stage be accessible to all. The Spirit gives gifts to all of God's people for the edification of the church. Some of those giftings are often exercised on the stage, and if a stage is not accessible and someone with a disability possesses one of those gifts typically expressed from the stage, then that person struggles to freely employ their gifting and the church loses out on a gift intended to strengthen it. For example, if someone with a wheelchair is asked to read Scripture, a teaching elder with a mobility challenge wants to deliver the message, or a congregation member desires to sing in the church praise band, they need access to the stage. Those people need to be able to participate as fully as possible and under as many of the same conditions as possible as those people without disabilities who contribute to the church via those roles.

Sometimes stage access can be achieved through creative workarounds. For example, sometimes a plank of wood is enough to generate a makeshift ramp. Other times there is backstage access that is often not considered. When constructing a new stage, access should be considered not just for handlers but for assets as well. In fact, for my (Jason's) capstone seminary preaching course, the classroom I was assigned to previously did not have a stage. They added a stage the summer before I took the class to add a degree of realistic simulation. This newly added change, however, made what would have been completely accessible for me inaccessible. When constructing the stage, they could have easily added a ramp. However, in my final semester, the school added that small stage to create the experience of preaching above people but didn't consider people like me when doing so. The new stage was completely inaccessible.

It is important when new buildings are going up that these elements be considered or, in the case of an older church, to strategize with the individual assets as to how access to the stage might be achieved. Always remember in the grand scheme of things, access does not have to be ADA compliant so long as the asset is able to access it. You may not be able to make something ADA compliant, but you can at least make it so the asset can participate.

Coffee

The coffee bar can play a huge role in fostering fellowship in the life of the church. Coffee and a cluster of people munching on a particular church's snack of choice offers a warm and relaxed environment. However, that environment is sometimes unwelcoming toward people with disabilities. Maybe the coffee bar is a high-top bar so that the coffee and other assorted goodies are out of reach for a person using a wheelchair. Perhaps sufficient seating is not offered in the immediate vicinity of the coffee bar so those with ambulatory disabilities who need to sit while they drink coffee cannot remain inside the center of all the fellowship.

Churches need to assess whether their fellowship spaces offer a warm, inclusive space or yet another space that requires so much energy and effort to navigate and inhabit that it fails to be welcoming. For coffee bars and cafés, it is important for potential handlers to be observant as to potential needs. If you observe someone who is standing far off and looking unsure, approach and engage, kindly asking if they need assistance.

Assets typically don't have a problem asking, but sometimes it is difficult for us to get people's attention. Sometimes this is because of having to break through what I call the "clotting effect," where small groups of people are clustered together, isolated in their own world and oblivious to what is going on around them. Sometimes the asset might not ask for help as a test to see how welcoming the environment might be. Asking someone if they need help, even if they do not, demonstrates your concern and care. Asking allows the asset to make known their individual preference.

Perception: Ryan's Story

Don't assume that disabilities look alike. Putting every person with a disability in the same bucket assumes that all people with disabilities experience the same thing. PWDs possess just as wide a variety of desires as people without disabilities. For example, my son sometimes prefers attending my life group because it treats him like everyone else. His disability remains unique from the disabilities that others face, and the church needs to recognize that, in order to best minister to my son and other people with disabilities, the church must see them as individuals.

Sacraments

During his first advent, Christ ordained two sacraments: communion and baptism. Every believer, and hence every member of Christ's body, is to partake of those undisputed sacraments. As such, they must be accessible to all believers.

Churches practice communion in a wide variety of ways. Some churches pass trays holding the bread and wine or grape juice while others invite congregants to come forward to receive the elements. Regardless of the methods involved, the church must ensure people with disabilities are able to engage with the rest of the congregation as the whole church partakes in the Lord's Supper. If trays are passed, those trays need to be manageable by those with disabilities, or other congregant members or those passing the elements need to be ready to step up to assist brothers and sisters with disabilities so they can participate in the church's communal meal.

If the congregation goes forward to receive the elements, the people who distribute the elements need a system to find and then deliver the meal to those PWDs who cannot go forward. Space and time also need to be allocated for those people with disabilities who do have the capacity to go forward. Whatever accommodation needs to be made to support them and their mobility devices, those adjustments should be made.

Some churches ask you to hold the elements for an extended period, which can be difficult for a person with a disability. In fact, there have been multiple times when I (Jason) was holding the grape juice, praying I would be able to hold it steady for what seemed like an eternity! In such cases, consider having the people distributing the elements ask individuals if they need assistance. Most of the time when the elements are distributed, the ushers move on without pausing to ask or even giving the opportunity for the asset to ask. It could also be helpful to mention the process of communion before the elements are handed out and to mention, "If anyone needs assistance feel free to ask an usher," making it clear assistance is available.

Churches also practice baptism in a wide variety of ways. However a church decides to practice baptism, it must be understood that various methods and modes of baptism remain available to all—people with and without disabilities. For churches and parishes holding to believer's baptism or the baptism of people old enough to make an informed decision regarding baptism, those churches need to provide accessible avenues toward baptism.

If a church provides baptismal facilities, they ought to be made accessible. For example, if a church has a baptismal built into a stage, the stage needs to be made accessible and appropriate grab bars ought to be installed on either side of the stairs that lead down into the water. If a church congregates somewhere outside the church building, conducting baptisms at a pool or lake for instance, someone needs to conduct a reconnaissance mission to make sure it is possible for people with disabilities to access that site whether they are getting baptized or supporting others in the church who are receiving baptism. If a church practices baptism by immersion, a church needs to consider and address whether a person's disability or the equipment necessary to support the person with a disability means that person cannot experience baptism by immersion.

The church may want to figure out a way to make it known other options are available if needed while also considering how to make that specific, individual baptism as seamless as possible from the normative baptismal process in that church. Because people's disabilities vary, the physicality of the process of baptism may require a prior conversation. Again, like all the other aspects, friendship trumps physical accessibility.

When I (Jason) was baptized, the church I was attending at the time had no baptismal facilities. We baptized people in a yard bucket. Normally, the person being baptized would climb in and be dunked. However, I was not able to climb in. But since I had a conversation with the pastor, we were able to create a meaningful experience where several people lifted me up and dunked me in the bucket. It felt like I was the paraplegic when his friends were lowering him on the mat to see Jesus. If my fellow congregants had not been willing, I never would have been able to be baptized and therefore would not have been obedient to Christ's command.

Baptism requires a conversation which is dependent upon the number of people willing to help and what the asset feels comfortable with. In that situation, I did not offer the solution—the pastor did. It is particularly refreshing for an asset when others can produce out-of-the-box ideas. This removes from assets the tremendous amount of pressure they constantly feel from being forced to be the only ones advocating for themselves.

Speakers

For individuals with high sensitivity to sound, loud music and sermons can be agitating. Having headphones for children and adults available at a tech booth or the welcome center can help muffle the noise and make the worship service accessible to everyone.

If your church uses hymnals, consider having copies of the individual music for those who have difficulty physically manipulating the books. In addition, consider providing a PowerPoint slide, transcript, or an interpreter for those deaf or hard of hearing. An enlarged copy of the music might also be helpful for those with visual impairments. Again, you do not need to have all these solutions on hand, but you should be willing to listen and learn and have these conversations with the asset.

Providing accessible facilities is the first step to making church a house of prayer for all people. However, creating an accessible and welcoming culture is just as important. In the next chapter, we examine social barriers which hinder many PWDs from experiencing the blessing of full fellowship.

Chapter 3

SOCIAL BARRIERS

MISSING MEMBERS

Who doesn't enjoy watching America's favorite pastime, baseball? Many in the United States cling to America's classic sport as a vestige of a simpler era. They reminisce about hot dogs and mustard stains, the pitcher-hitter showdown and team chants, cracking bats and the home-run ball they caught when they were twelve years old. Critics remind us that bright lights, television, and runaway salaries have almost ruined the game. By the time you read this, a player will have signed a twenty-year, one-billion-dollar contract—an off-putting deal for alienated, long-suffering fans who remember the simpler times.

Nine players make up a baseball team's starting lineup: a catcher, pitcher, first baseman, second baseman, shortstop, third baseman, left fielder, center fielder, and right fielder. While the multi-role team plays defense on the field, the nine opposing players file up to home plate. The opposing players, the batters, take their turn, hoping to hit the ball and score runs. Just as there are nine starting players on each team, each game contains nine innings. Excitement runs higher when the teams approach the final inning with a close score. Fans watch, comparing the number of strikes to balls and crossing their fingers for a run. Tensions mount in the last inning or two as the final few pitchers and batters vie to see which team will win the game.

Imagine the scenario. Everyone's expecting their favorite baseball team to enjoy a winning season. Reports leak out of spring training that this just might be the year the team wins it all—taking home the World Series trophy! Opening Day approaches, and optimism peaks as you settle in for the season-long chase to secure the pennant. You break out your T-shirts and switch your profile picture to one of you and your family at the ballpark. But then, a few days before opening day, you hear an unwelcome news report: the team's two first basemen were injured in a motorcycle accident. Your team was so confident in the professional abilities of those two highly skilled, and now injured, players that they failed to draft or develop any other first basemen. That World Series pennant you hoped to hang in your office turns into an impossible reality. The players are headed into the season with *no one* covering first base.

You hope for the best, but deep down you cannot imagine how the team will ever possibly cover the massive gap down the first base line. You have heard that both the pitcher and the catcher have received instructions to sprint toward first base whenever necessary. That plan will wear your pitcher ragged and distract him from his major focus, working the tension he teases out with the hitter. The second baseman was told to scoot halfway down the line toward first base. Knowing that one-ninth of the team will not be on the field, even the right fielder has been instructed to move in toward first base. Hitting a high fly ball—an easy out in most scenarios—might prove successful for a hitter.

Have the managers implemented strategies due to the loss of their two first basemen? Yes. But their strategies will not stand up. They scream in desperation. The season starts, and your optimism wanes. It is Opening Day, and you might as well hand all the opposing hitters a walk to first base. You know in your head and in your heart you are facing a terrible season with no one covering first base!

Of course, your instincts prove correct. Everyone in the country is talking about *the team with no first baseman*. It is not enough knowing most hitters will make it to second base with ease. You hear about it constantly on the radio—*the baseball team without a first baseman.* The losses begin piling up. Even though the manager protests there wasn't anything he could do to prevent the motorcycle accident, the owners fire him for not having the team ready to begin the season and not having backups in place. Not having a first baseman has crippled your team. They limp through the season. The players wear out faster and their focus is not on their roles as they try to cope without the first baseman. The team is crushed. The fans are wounded. How many seasons until people forget this incident? Will it ever be forgotten? Who knows how long it will take for the entire city to heal?

Why are so many churches trying to play without a first baseman? People with disabilities make up 20 percent of the American population. Churches that exclude those with disabilities find themselves down a first baseman (and a catcher, too). This attitude is one of the largest social barriers preventing full inclusion of PWDs within our churches.

Of course, not having a first baseman on a baseball team is unthinkable. But many of us are okay with a shortage of people with a disability using their gifts in the body of Christ. If you walk into a baseball stadium and there is no player at first base, it won't take long to notice. But how many times have you walked into a large sanctuary, looked at the beautiful, carpet-covered steps leading up to the choir loft, and thought, "I wonder how a person in a wheelchair gets up there?"

If this lack of involvement were simply a preference, it might be less grievous. We normally prefer hearing the gifted singers leading us into worship and eloquent speakers expounding on the text. And how much better if the folks on the stage also happen to be smiling, beautiful, and fashionable. Those on the stage or serving in leadership positions surely represent the rest of us, and we want to have those kinds of people (smiling, beautiful, and fashionable) represent us. We like what we see, and the beautiful people make us feel better about ourselves and our God. We surmise our neighbors and friends will feel good about attending as well. Like teens at their lunchroom tables, we want to be part of a popular church, part of a church that looks a certain way.

The Two Sides of the Same Coin:
Darryl and Kasey's Story of Searching for a New Church

What's the first piece of advice given to every seminary student? "Look for a new church home close to your seminary so that you can serve the local church and receive support from that local church throughout the duration of your studies." As soon as we entered seminary, we followed that advice. We started the hunt, excited to explore all the churches offered in the big city. It took almost no time for us to realize this pattern: how a church treated our son with special needs provided an excellent insight into a church's heart. How a church treated our son revealed the true atmosphere of any church.

At first, we thought church size might influence how a church interacted with our son, but size turned out to be less of a factor than we thought. The number of available resources also turned out to be less of a big deal than we thought. The availability of resources didn't necessarily translate to a guaranteed fit. We visited small churches filled with people who housed plenty of space in their hearts for our son, and we visited large churches overflowing with tons of people who served on ministry teams. However, those teams lacked ideas on how to minister to our son.

Around the time our son turned six years old, one of the larger churches scolded us. They told us they'd put our son in the nursery the next time we attended. That next time never arrived. Sometimes we received special parking spots and date nights without ever feeling welcomed into a congregation. We encountered an interesting dynamic: two sides of the same coin. For example, if the children's ministry felt plastic and distant, the adult side of the church felt plastic and distant too. If a warm welcome saturated the adult service, no matter the size, most of the time the children's church offered a warm welcome too.

Prayer proved key throughout our many church-search adventures. God knew our family, and he knew the church that he longed for all of us to call home.

The problem is we sometimes view certain people as "less than" or "other." If someone is too old, well, we should replace them with a younger person. If someone is physically disabled, we might not have the patience to hear them speak or teach. If someone with an intellectual disability wants to join the choir, we are quick to list reasons why this just is not *practical*. And yet, as the apostle Paul reminds us, all are needed in the body of Christ:

> For the body is not one part, but many. If the foot says, "Because I am not a hand, I am not a part of the body," it is not for this reason any less a part of the body. And if the ear says, "Because I am not an eye, I am not a part of the body," it is not for this reason any less a part of the body. If the whole body were an eye, where would the hearing be? If the whole body were hearing, where would the sense of smell be? But now God has arranged the parts, each one of them in the body, just as He desired. If they were all one part, where would the body be? But now there are many parts, but one body. And the eye cannot say to the hand, "I have no need of you"; or again, the head to the feet, "I have no need of you." On the contrary, it is much truer that the parts of the body which seem to be weaker are necessary; and those parts of the body which we consider less honorable, on these we bestow greater honor, and our less presentable parts become much more presentable, whereas our more presentable parts have no need of it. But God has so composed the body, giving more abundant honor to that part which lacked, so that there may be no division in the body, but that the parts may have the same care for one another. And if one part of the body suffers, all the parts suffer with it; if a part is honored, all the parts rejoice with it. Now you are Christ's body, and individually parts of it. (1 Cor. 12:14–27 NASB)

TEN COMMON SOCIAL BARRIERS
Physical barriers to inclusivity are often easier to see than social ones. Doorways can be measured, and stairwells can be counted. Once

you make sure that you meet the standards, you can check off the box that reads "accessible." Yet, if you look around and see only non-disabled people in your church, you may as well be missing a first baseman.

In our discussions, we have found it is better for a church to be mind-set accessible than facility accessible. Mindset accessibility takes continual effort, assessment, and readjustment. It is not like a ramp you install or headset devices you order. In our research, we have run up against ten common social barriers (or excuses) to including those with disabilities in the local church community. Which ones do you identify with?

1. "I might do or say something offensive, and I do not want to hurt this person."
2. "We do not fully understand all they are going through and legitimately do not know how we might help. In fact, we might make their condition worse."
3. "I fear getting involved with this person may begin to dominate my time, schedule, and work-life balance."
4. "This person has their own family and friends. What could I add to the relationship? I have never been trained to help someone with a disability!"
5. "This person seems needy. If we build a friendship, it will involve endless car rides to the doctor's office and assisting them in their everyday activities."
6. "We are not good with medical issues such as giving shots, helping with seizures, or changing colostomy bags. We are leaving this relationship with the doctors and nurses!"
7. "We have a few close friends. We are not sure they will want to hang out with us if we make new friends with disabilities."
8. "We would bring a person with a disability to our church, but we have absolutely zero ministry activities targeted toward this demographic. We are not sure they would feel welcome."
9. "We would build a friendship with a person with a disability, but we are already heavily involved in another ministry at our fellowship."
10. "We do not know any people with disabilities in our community."

Of these ten social barriers, all but one include an element of fear—number 10 being the lone exception. The largest social barrier to including those in the disability community in the life of the church is fear: fear of being excluded, insufficient, or overworked. But we are told in Scripture that perfect love casts out fear (1 John 4:18). We are forced to deal with honest questions: Do I really love the person with a disability, or do I love my convenience? Do I love serving someone with a physical disability, or do I prefer my own comfort?

Because we (the authors) hold to the social model of disability, our primary focus is overcoming social barriers. The main reason for this? Even if all the physical barriers are removed, a person with a disability could still feel isolated and unwelcome. On the other side, if the social barriers are removed, oftentimes physical barriers can be mitigated in creative ways. Another reason we are choosing to focus on social barriers? Many churches have tight budgets and understandably do not have the cash flow to make the necessary physical renovations. However, it does not cost any money to be a genuine and caring friend.

A PERSONAL INCONVENIENCE

I (Paul) have never forgotten the many lifelong lessons I learned from a blind woman I will call Gwen. Our family would often pick Gwen up on Sundays as we rode to our church's worship services. As a bratty child I sometimes viewed this assistance as an inconvenience. "Isn't there a service that can do this?" I wondered. Since that time, I have learned that families like ours, people helping people, oftentimes provide the only available help.

Sure, we picked up Gwen from her apartment, but one of us would also be asked to walk to her front door and ring the bell. In Topeka, Kansas, the winters are often brutally cold. You can imagine the response from a selfish kid being asked to stand on the front porch in the snow waiting for blind Gwen to emerge. Let us just say this was before the days of the plastic bracelets proclaiming WWJD (What Would Jesus Do?).

Looking back, I cannot imagine what I was thinking! Was Gwen expected to walk alone down several miles to our church building? Even if it were not "Kansas cold" outside, could she have been expected to see and avoid the ice on the road or navigate the piles of snow the road graders had pushed to the side of the street? Selfishly I thought, "I could have walked to church—what was hindering Gwen?"

Thankfully, our family did more than simply offer rides. Over time Gwen was asked whether she could come to our home for lunch or go with us to a restaurant. She would come to our home after church worship service to simply sit and visit.

I remember the time she patiently explained to me how she carefully handled her money. Gwen explained the coins were, thankfully, each a distinct size. In this way a dime was seldom confused with a quarter. But what about the paper bills? She told us many in the blind community fold their bills in special ways to not mix up a one-dollar bill with a twenty-dollar bill. We realized in those teachable moments how vulnerable some disabilities leave us. Imagine someone giving a blind person a one-dollar bill and telling them it was a twenty! It happens.

I also remember being surprised one afternoon to finally notice Gwen wearing a wristwatch. "Why do you wear a watch?" I blurted. "You can't even see it!" She laughed and showed how she opened the glass covering the top while carefully running her fingers over the face. Like many blind and visually impaired people, Gwen used a "hands-on" tactile watch. This was long before the days of talking watches which some in the blind community have adopted. Even now, I am told, many blind and visually impaired prefer tactile watches. Since I often preach and teach, I am grateful that a room full of computer voices does not start alerting the wearers we have sailed past the intended closing time of the worship service!

Stealing french fries from someone's plate is common among most families. So you can imagine how surprised I was when I was busted by none other than . . . you guessed it, Gwen! We were at a sit-down restaurant with our family of five plus Gwen around the table. As a selfish teenager, I wanted to hurry through dinner and get on with my own schedule. After inhaling my dinner, I glanced over at Gwen's plate and noticed she had lots of french fries left. Rudely, I began stealing fries off her plate.

"I believe someone has been taking my french fries," Gwen said calmly. But how could she know? And, who? I thought my crime was unsolvable. Of course my brother, or maybe it was my sister, shrieked,

"It was Paul!" "I thought so," said Gwen. "He is sitting here, on my right side. And I noticed my pile of fries was getting smaller on the right side."

I was surprised, and we all had a good laugh. But the lesson was learned. Gwen was a person. She was fully human. As a selfish, inward-focused child, I viewed Gwen with pity. I saw her as a *project* we might be able to help or solve, or as a lady who was a burden. And yet, over time, and because of my parents' patience, I began to see Gwen as a friend. Once, when we were watching television, I sheepishly offered, "What do *you* want to watch, Gwen?" She said, "Oh it doesn't really matter . . . I mostly enjoy hearing your reactions and listening to your conversations." I thought of how often Gwen must have sat . . . alone . . . in her apartment. I thought of how I always took my ability to *see* for granted. I imagined playing my favorite sport, golf, as a person with blindness. I imagined my visual world going dark.

The more time I spent around Gwen, the more I began seeing what life was like for her. I began to closely observe how she adroitly used her folding, blind mobility cane, how well she had developed her senses of touch and hearing. I learned how to walk along at a normal pace while she gently held the back of my arm.

My own selfishness had initially hindered Gwen from becoming a friend. One of the strongest ways to clear the social barriers to full inclusion is to combat fear and selfishness, welcoming those with disabilities into friendships. Melinda Jones Ault's doctoral dissertation, which questioned more than 400 parents of children with disabilities involved in faith communities, noted that "more than 90 percent of church-going special needs parents cited the most helpful support to be a 'welcoming attitude toward people with disabilities.'"[1]

"DISABILITY DISTRICTS"

For far too long, people with disabilities have visited our churches and fellowships and been told, "Oh, we see you have a person with a disability in your family. You should come on Tuesday night! That is the

---

1. Melinda Jones Ault, "Participation of Families of Children with Disabilities in Their Faith Communities: A Survey of Parents" (PhD diss., University of Kentucky, 2010), 81.

night we do ministry for our members with disabilities." Potential key players have been shoved into boxes that keep them from participating as full members of the team . . . that is, the church.

Imagine if at the beginning of a worship service the pastor called everyone with a pet fish to the front of the sanctuary. It did not matter if the pet was a goldfish, betta fish, or shark. Everyone with a pet fish was then taken away to a "special room" for "appropriate programming." The audience would talk among themselves. "What is wrong with them?" "Are they okay?" and "Glad I don't have a fish!"

Whether sectioned into separate rooms or relegated to a different night, too many disability ministries turn into disability districts, where those who are deemed nonnormative are sectioned into their own segment away from the general population. Those with physical disabilities are often ushered into the disability classroom whether they want to be there or not.

One of the major problems with the disability district is that it does not allow for individual tailoring among the participants. All attendees are forced to function at the lowest common denominator, so even if a person could carry on an intelligent conversation, by the very nature and culture of the room they are often stifled, even bored, with nothing to do. This was my (Jason's) experience with many disability camps. I was often one of the most "normal" people there. I dreaded attending special classrooms or events because I knew I would not fit in. Even to this day, I shudder when someone suggests that I should participate in a disability classroom or ministry.

Another major problem with corralling all the people with disabilities into a type of disability district is that it betrays often unspoken, inaccurate worldviews:

- "People with a disability are not made in the image of God." While we give tacit mental assent to the truthful idea they are human, our actions subtly betray the faulty mindset that they are not fully human. "They need to be in their own group."
- "People with a disability are more trouble than they are worth." We believe we can effectively undertake ministry for normal people. But we think it takes too much time, resources, and effort

to do ministry for folks with disabilities. We forget the apostle Paul said, "I can do all things through Christ who strengthens me" (Phil. 4:13 NKJV).

- "People with disabilities are less human than I am!" This false mindset expresses itself in saying things like, "I can minister to them . . . but how could they ever minister to me?"
- "People with a disability are a legal liability to a local church. If we attempt to minister to them and someone is injured or falls, we could be sued." This argument is rarely made with others in the church.
- "People with a disability cannot fully enter into worship." This faulty mindset is owing to the misconception there is only one correct way to worship.
- "People with a disability cannot use their gifts." Some think PWDs either do not possess gifts or are incapable of using them. Others admit, "We do not know how to allow them to use their gifts."
- "People with a disability need to be cordoned off with others who also have a disability." This implies non-disabled members and handlers could never receive encouragement or benefit from the gifts of persons with a disability.
- "People with a disability always disrupt the worship service and make visitors feel uncomfortable." But are visitors more important than members with disabilities? And perhaps visitors would be encouraged to see active participation from all the members!
- "People with disabilities are needy and require extra time." Did Jesus not say, "apart from me you can do nothing" (John 15:5)? Somewhere along the way, we elevated efficiency and expediency above authentic lived experience. Have we learned to worship and undertake ministry with key members of our body absent?

Finally, the worst part of accidentally (or intentionally) building a disability district is the way each group is cordoned off from the other, so we all miss the blessing of being full participants in God's family. Since there is only one body, we need to interact with all its members. There is one body, one Spirit.

This leads us to our next point. After avoiding disability districts, our research revealed that providing support for children to participate in regular activities is critical for families to feel welcomed by a church. Seventy percent of parents indicated that inclusion in regular activities was important, yet less than 30 percent of parents felt that their church offered that support.[2]

The goal is for everyone to become a part of the beloved community. This is a tremendous goal for all churches, parishes, parachurch organizations, and nonprofit groups. As you continue to perform audits on your church's best practices (see Chapter 6), stop and ask, "Are there those in our number we may not be fully welcoming? Are any of my friends with disabilities feeling isolated or finding themselves out of touch with what's happening with other members?" Do you sometimes see people who are on the periphery of your ministry? Hopefully, prayerfully, you are always reaching out with the love of Jesus to welcome them into your growing, beloved community.

Finally, we want to make mention of realities that impact both those with and without disabilities. We have all been affected by the fall. Our humanity was effaced, but not erased. We each possess the imago Dei (the image of God). However, sin has limited our effectiveness. There are no perfect people in the body of Christ. Thus, after spending time looking into the needs of the disability community, we next turn the magnifying glass inward.

By taking this turn we realize even our best able-bodied abilities are not our own, but are gracious gifts given from the hand of our loving God. In addition, our non-disabled mindset sometimes allows us to think we are using our gifts and undertaking honorable deeds in our own strength. Again, we fail to remember Jesus's words, "apart from me you can do nothing" (John 15:5). Jesus taught the great and gifted apostle Paul this invaluable truth: "My grace is sufficient for you, for my power is made perfect in weakness" (2 Cor. 12:9a). This reminds us we also have our own set of dis-abilities.

We know some local fellowships are flourishing as they minister for and alongside people with disabilities. We also understand that many

---

2. Ault, "Participation of Families of Children with Disabilities in Their Faith Communities," 81.

local churches need encouragement in this area. The problem is that full inclusivity for PWDs may feel overwhelming. And rightly so. That problem presents a great need involving a lot of our brothers and sisters in Christ and has gone widely unaddressed. However, when we understand our ever-present need to allow God to work on our own dis-abilities, we gain a more realistic glimpse into our desperate need to work toward full inclusivity for PWDs. We hope you see the great need facing the church and the need to work toward a solution that leads to the full inclusion of people with disabilities in our faith communities.

MINISTRY PERFORMED *WITH* AND *BY* PWDS

Strategic conversations need to continue to take place surrounding the barriers most PWDs face when they express a desire to serve. We have articulated some of the physical barriers to ministry inclusion and involvement, and we have also addressed the many social barriers our friends with disabilities face when they enter the ministerial arena. We need to explore practical solutions to help them navigate these social barriers so they can effectively serve.

When people with disabilities ask to serve in ministry, there are typically three general responses expressed; two negative and one positive. One, there is a *pay-your-dues* approach many churches employ. To be considered for volunteering or service, a person has to demonstrate they are dedicated, which would then lead to more opportunities. For example, assisting the praise band or serving with the audio-visual team often leads to being given higher responsibilities like teaching or leading a small group. However, often these entry-level ministry positions are out of reach for many with disabilities. They cannot physically perform on stage or operate much of the sophisticated audio-visual equipment.

In some senses, even serving on the greeting team might be out of reach because the main purpose of the greeter is to bridge the gap between someone who is new and those in the established community. But if someone is already feeling isolated, the best that person can do as a greeter is say, "I am glad you are here! I do not know anyone, so let us be lonely together!" This is not a good situation for greeting. This creates a self-perpetuating spiral where the assets are not able to prove themselves in the entry-level positions and therefore do not receive any higher-level serving or volunteer opportunities, rendering service in this system a near impossibility.

Another possibility is that a service opportunity is given, but is primarily offered out of pity, not necessarily out of need. One time when I (Jason) went on a service trip with my church, one of the jobs I was given was to help paint a post. I spent the better part of an hour and a half expending all my energy trying to effectively paint the post. The moment I finished, someone came along behind me and in a matter of thirty seconds went over the entire post and the sections I missed. This made me feel I was only given this opportunity out of pity because I asked, not because they wanted me to help or that I possessed expertise in this area. In fact, it felt like they did not want me to do the task anyway.

The third possibility is the one positive response, which admittedly takes a considerable amount of work. Essentially, it is a dialogue between the leadership and the asset. Oftentimes in this situation the handler might perform the role of advocate for the asset. But regardless of how the conversation is initiated, it centers around realistically discussing the asset's limitations, abilities, and giftedness. Coming alongside this important step should be a plan or at least an observation of the asset being faithful in the opportunities provided. The asset should be given responsibility within the field of what they can realistically undertake. As they are successful, they should be given more responsibility. For example, if their spiritual gift is in the area of teaching, have them begin by mentoring someone one-on-one under observation, then perhaps teaching to a small group of three or five, and finally teaching to a classroom filled with learners. This way, they can demonstrate they are both faithful and equipped for the work.

Related to this, it is also helpful to have a clear track for someone to follow (or shadow) if they desire to do a particular type of ministry. Often in our churches, particularly with teaching, there exists a philosophy of "you will randomly fall into it" or getting the position if you schmooze enough with the current teacher (which is a subset of the first negative reality we observed). This is especially frustrating for people who are physically disabled but not necessarily mentally disabled.

This reality creates a feeling that even if the person with disabilities is continually present and faithfully doing the tasks they are able to perform, they still can be stuck in a rut without any opportunities to exercise their spiritual gifts. Sometimes when I (Jason) have raised this issue with people and mention the vicious cycle of not being able to serve because I am unnoticed, they simply respond, "Well, you have to gain the church's trust before they give you any high-caliber opportunities." While I do not deny this fact, the people I talked to view this barrier as necessary to preserve the church's integrity, instead of thinking of alternative ways to establish trust. In fact, this sentiment was echoed by the head of the disability department at one of my schools—the person who arranged my accommodations and was supposed to be my advocate!

I have observed this reality in some churches who assert they want *everyone* to serve, stating, "There is a place of service for everyone here!" But if I ask if there is anything I can do or help with, the only response I receive is blank stares or the repeated phrase, "Something will come up," but with no concrete plan of action. This response could be influenced by a desire for efficiency. More likely, it indicates a lack of a desire for thinking freely or putting in the necessary work. Churches are sometimes insurance risk-assessors who reason, "It is not worth it to put in the additional effort and thought process for the asset to serve in our community." This is completely opposite to Jesus's approach, since he often went out of his way to minister to those with physical disabilities.

People with disabilities need to know unrealistic optimism often becomes a path to failure. We can help persons with a disability claim ownership of their desire to live out of their giftedness by simply acknowledging potential pitfalls and then exploring strategies to enhance their servant leadership skills. No one who engages in ministry or service to others does so perfectly. But we can undertake service activities in a healthy and effective manner. We can learn best practices from those who are actively engaged in this noble endeavor. All Christians (one body) should be encouraged to serve others in the power of the Holy Spirit (one Spirit) and faithfully use their unique gifts.

Disability researcher Erik Carter has established several of what he labels *portraits of community*—snapshots into different potential attitudes communities can have toward PWDs. They are exclusion, separation, integration, inclusion, and belonging. In the exclusion stage, people with disabilities are not even considered or known. At the separation stage, which he calls "ministry to," there are specific ministries designed for PWDs. However, this is purely seen as an outreach and can typically be sporadic, little more than checking off the box. His next portrait is integration or "ministry among," where PWDs are engaged with the standard experiences, like worship services, of a church or organization. At the integration stage, people with disabilities may be part of some activities but excluded from others. Inclusion is labeled "ministry with," where the people with intellectual disabilities are encouraged to participate in the activities without any distinction between those with and those without disabilities. Finally, belonging is an optimal state where every person in the community knows they belong and are fully valued.[3]

These five portraits are extremely helpful when determining where a church or organization is currently situated along the continuum of community building. In our opinion, Carter does not clearly communicate specifically *how* one moves from one stage to the next. It is *this* element we hope to articulate in the remaining chapters. Our model centers around five steps for disability ministry: notice, engage, research, incorporate, and advocate. We explore these concepts in detail in part 3 of this book. For now, let us offer a brief preview of the way our five steps of building a friendship with a person with a disability in some way mirrors Carter's.

Our first step is called Notice, where nothing is known about the person and more information needs to be gathered. This falls in between Dr. Carter's stage 1 and stage 2 of exclusion and separation. Our second step, Engage, falls between his second and third stages, separation and integration, where the handler is learning more about the asset. Our third step, Research, then makes Carter's fourth step, inclusion, possible. Our fourth step, Incorporate, mirrors Carter's inclusion very nicely, where the asset is becoming a part of and engaging with the community. Belonging is what occurs at our final step of Advocate, where the person with the disability feels that they can trust the handler and the community.

---

3.   Erik Carter, "The Changing Landscape of Disability and Ministry in the Church," *Currents in Theology and Mission* 49, no. 3 (2022): 4–9.

There is, however, one notable difference between our schema and Carter's. Ours focuses on a bottom-up approach. This is necessary because people with disabilities have varying needs and concerns and cannot all be quarantined into one section. Because of this, the relationship needs to develop on an individual level and then bloom to the organizational level. This approach also allows the mindset of the handler to be always looking to move the individual asset toward the belonging stage. The process starts over with each new asset. However, the more the process is repeated, the more a culture of belonging, to use Carter's term, is created. As leadership experts note, culture eats strategy for breakfast! In other words, a church or ministry can *say* they have a specific strategy to partner with those with disabilities; however, if a welcoming culture of inclusion fails to become part of the very culture of the organization, the strategies are simply words on a plaque.

In short, Dr. Carter shows us *where* we should go; our Five-Step Plan shows *how* to get there. While Carter's focus has mostly centered on those with intellectual disabilities, his system applies to people with physical disabilities as well. With some modifications, the Five-Step Plan we advocate can also be applied to people with intellectual disabilities. It just may take a greater degree of effort and further reliance upon the power of the Holy Spirit. *One Body, One Spirit* is offered for men and women who advocate incorporating more people with a disability into the life and service of a local church, parish, Christian school, or nonprofit organization. Further, our work encourages those with a disability who desire to serve and lead within the church to be enthusiastically allowed to do so. When our friends with disabilities are educated about the social obstacles they face and are given practical guides—and authentic friends—to steer around those obstacles, their opportunity for faithful success in ministry dramatically increases.

One of the unique purposes of this book is to describe those challenges, explain solutions, and encourage people with disabilities to faithfully minister. We aim to help break down the many social barriers those in the disability community face when they desire to serve God. The church has largely failed to acknowledge not only the unique giftedness of PWDs but also their very humanity. How else can you describe someone meeting a person with a disability and subsequently thinking aloud, "I cannot imagine any place in this church where they could serve"? And yet we continue to overhear this jaded response. A different statement needs to leap out of our mouths: "I cannot imagine a church without their acts of service!"

In fact, one of the effects we hope this book brings about is a broadening of mindset. While preparing this book we held conversations with many people and discovered something interesting. Those expressing the most positive reactions are those who in some way, shape, or form have been affected by PWDs. Maybe they have a brother, sister, family member, or friend with a disability. It is the exposure to this person with a disability that enables them to positively interact with others. We heard this sentiment expressed in many of our interviews.

We hope this book can function as a type of initial point of contact so that when you encounter a person with a disability in your community, you are primed and ready to establish authentic genuine friendships. This book is more for the inexperienced than it is for the veteran. Our hope and prayer is that we answer many of the questions and concerns you might have toward ministering to people with disabilities. We trust that an ever-increasing number of volunteers will embody Christ's attitude and work through the sometimes fearful or uncomfortable feelings that often accompany creating new friendships.

How are persons with disabilities welcomed into your midst? Are they seen as a blessing or a burden? What social barriers keep people from undertaking service to, with, and by friends with disabilities? Moving forward, we advocate for a practical step anyone can undertake to better welcome a person with a disability into your circle of influence. Let us all become bridge builders, helping those who struggle more than most. God's heart is for the physical, mental, and social struggler. As we close part 1, we trust you are convinced there are unmet ministry opportunities in and among the disability community. Often those on the "outside" can better see the blind spots in the church. Historical precedents, physical facilities, and social norms have made churches often inaccessible to those with disabilities. What are the viable, achievable solutions?

Part 2

BIBLICAL SOLUTIONS

Chapter 4

DISABILITY IN THE OLD TESTAMENT

Sometimes a gap seems to exist between the Old Testament and the New Testament. Since the heretic Marcion of Sinope, who argued Jesus was a new, loving God in contrast to the evil, vindictive God of the Old Testament, readers have wondered, "Is God's character really consistent between the first thirty-nine books of the Bible and the last twenty-seven?"

Regarding people with disabilities, we see strict purity laws in the Old Testament and sometimes occasional statements forbidding PWDs from ministering before God (Lev. 21:16–23), which could be misunderstood as God not caring for people with disabilities. On the other hand, we see Jesus's ministry focusing on PWDs: healing, helping, and ministering to them. On the surface, this would appear to be a stark contrast. In Malachi, God the Father declared his immutability (Mal. 3:6); Hebrews insists that Jesus's ministry was the continuation and fulfillment of God's plan (Heb. 6:17–20). If God has not changed, why are the Mosaic law and Levitical requirements so harsh against PWDs?

Did God care for people with disabilities when he delivered the law to Moses or during the times of the kings? Accounts relating the stories of PWDs occur with a higher frequency throughout the Gospels and the Acts of the Apostles, and those writings convey a tenderness toward people with disabilities that does not appear quite as readily in the Old Testament. Does God's concern for PWDs exist in the Old Testament, or is that solely a New Testament concern?

In Exodus 34 when God meets Moses on the mountain a second time, after the golden calf incident, God inscribes a second set of tablets with the Ten Commandments. Prior to writing on the tablets, God declared himself to be "the LORD, the LORD, a God merciful and gracious, slow to anger, and abounding in steadfast love and faithfulness, keeping steadfast love for thousands, forgiving iniquity and transgression and sin, but who will by no means clear the guilty, visiting the iniquity of the fathers on the children and the children's children, to the third and the fourth generation" (Exod. 34:6–7).

God revealed himself as merciful and gracious, abounding in steadfast love and faithfulness, and forgiving. Christ models those traits to those with disabilities so clearly throughout the Gospels. But does the Old Testament portray God extending those character traits toward PWDs? Jesus embraced the blind, the crippled, and the mute, but was that tenderness always on God's heart? Does the posture that Jesus held and modeled for his church to hold toward PWDs align with God's posture toward people with disabilities in the Old Testament? Or does a disparity exist between the God revealed in the Old Testament and the God-man revealed through the incarnation? This chapter wrestles with these questions and seeks out God's heart regarding them by digging into the Word of God.

God's desire to heal the brokenness that resulted from the fall never wavered after the fall. He longs for us to experience the trajectory of redemption history. In the meantime, he has never stopped caring for those who are hurting due to the fall and its effects, and that love encompasses every person, including people with disabilities. God wants to heal the gap that exists between himself and the totality of his created order.

Through the Old Testament, God exposed the problem that separates him from humanity: humanity chose to rebel against a perfect God, and no form of imperfection can stand welcome before God (Hab. 1:13, Col. 1:21–22). Humankind possesses a desperate and very real need for someone who is perfect, who can make all things right, including the healing of the fallen creation, a healing that must cure all disabilities. When God sets up the problem as clearly as possible, humanity gains a fuller view of the reality of their desperate need for a Savior, and that need serves to propel humanity toward Christ and his waiting arms.

The Old Testament clarifies the need for the God-man and makes that need explicit. In addition to God's self-description in Exodus 34:6–7, God reveals the holiness of his character to his people, stating, "You shall be holy, for I the LORD your God am holy" (Lev. 19:2). God is holy, and his people must be holy too. There is a fittingness to God's holiness. It is right that he is holy, and it is right, or fitting, that his people be holy too. But his people cannot be holy. When people are left to their own devices, the fittingness required to be God's people remains totally removed from their grasp, a fittingness that cannot be achieved by the imperfect.

Imperfection marks the totality of the created order. No one is holy aside from God. That gives rise to the question, "Is anyone worthy?" That question points to humanity's deepest need, and God answers that there will be one who is worthy. The entirety of the Old Testament builds humanity's anticipation as God prepares the world for the arrival of the one who is worthy, the only one, the Lamb of God (Rev. 4:8–11; 5:8–14).

When compared with the New Testament, the Old Testament holds very few accounts telling the stories of people with disabilities. However, that disparity does not mean the Old Testament, or the God revealed in it, lacked care and compassion toward PWDs. The tenderness of God's heart toward those with disabilities still appears throughout the text.

To start, several Levitical laws guarded the defenseless. By extension, those laws potentially protected people with disabilities (Lev. 19:14; Deut. 27:18). While those laws do not tell the stories of PWDs, those laws direct God's people to make and maintain provisions for people with disabilities. Laws concerning gleaning, for example, ensured that the marginalized, widowed, and fatherless retained access to food. Those laws required the harvesters to leave the edges of the wheat fields untouched and the vineyard workers to pass over the fallen grapes and even some of the fruit still clinging to the vines, so the impoverished and the traveler might gather grain and grapes (Lev. 19:9–10).

While the laws on gleaning do not explicitly mention those with disabilities, those laws extended their protective covering over them. Other laws provided direct orders regarding people with disabilities, such as commands prohibiting God's people from holding contempt toward the deaf or putting an obstacle in front of the blind (Lev. 19:14). Additional laws ensured families retained their abilities to support and care for fellow family members (Lev. 25:25–55). For instance, the laws regarding the kinsman-redeemer and the reversion of the land back to the land's original owner in the Year of Jubilee allowed families to support themselves despite hardships (Lev. 25:25–28). If a family lost their land, the main source of life in the ancient Near East, the eventual redemption of that land always remained a possibility regardless of the circumstances surrounding the loss, including the occurrence of disabilities.

Those kinds of Old Testament laws ensured care for the otherwise overlooked and marginalized and revealed God's heart toward people with disabilities. Those laws portray God's tenderness and provision for people struggling against barriers—sometimes permanent barriers—threatening to bar those people from a flourishing life.

Occasionally, people suggest the law does not represent a tenderness toward PWDs, but an exclusion toward them. Those people view the law as partly cutting off those with disabilities, since people with disabilities from the tribe of Levi were not allowed to participate in the priesthood. In Leviticus 21:16–23, priests with blemishes or disabilities face prohibitions from making offerings to the Lord. The Law explicitly states, "No man of the offspring of Aaron the priest who has a blemish shall come near to offer the LORD's food offerings; since he has a blemish, he shall not come near to offer the bread of his God" (Lev. 21:21). Levites with defects and disabilities were not allowed to approach the altar.

Like the priests who made the offerings, the holy place and the offerings themselves had to be perfect. No blemishes were allowed. Imperfections would profane the sanctuary and the person who mediated the forgiveness fostered by the sacrificial system. That correlation between a perfect God and a temple, priests, and sacrifices without blemishes possesses a fittingness. It is right that a perfect God be approached by priests without blemish and receive sacrifices without blemish.

Despite the lack of blemishes on God's temple, his priests, and the sacrifices, all three failed to be perfect. Yet, despite that lack of holiness, God's mercy and grace reached out and found a way to declare God's people holy. Christ, the Perfect, came, touching people with disabilities and making explicit the need for the God-man, and Christ will come again to touch and forever heal every blemish.

Two well-known examples of people with disabilities occur in the Old Testament: Isaac and Mephibosheth. Genesis and 2 Samuel tell their stories and invite readers to witness how others treated those two assets. In the Genesis account, Jacob deceived his father. He took advantage of Isaac's blindness to steal the blessing from his older brother, Esau (Gen. 27:1–41). In 2 Samuel, the author tells of David's grief over Saul and Jonathan's deaths. David's sorrow compels him to seek out Jonathan's son, Mephibosheth, who experienced a crippling injury when he and his nurse fled after his father and grandfather fell in battle (1 Sam. 31:1–13; 2 Sam. 4:4; 9:1–13). Readers encounter a negative example in Jacob through his abuse of Isaac's blindness to achieve selfish gain, while David provides a more positive example through his care for Mephibosheth.

In Genesis 25, God told Rebekah she would bear two sons and the older would serve the younger (Gen. 25:23). Before he was even born, God had already decreed Jacob would receive the birthright, but Jacob took matters into his own hands—a strategy often implemented by the patriarchs when they failed to trust God's protection and provision (Gen. 12:10–20; 16:1–3; 20:1–18; 25:29–34; 26:6–11). Jacob abused his father's failing sight to strip the blessing away from Esau. Rather than trusting God to deliver on his promise, Jacob seized the blessing for himself via lies and manipulation.

The text does not condone Jacob's actions, nor does the text reveal that God sanctioned Jacob's self-chosen path to blessing. Later, when Laban deceived Jacob, and so deceived the deceiver, the text discloses the author's tone toward Jacob's deception. Laban changed Jacob's wages multiple times but, despite Laban's repeated attempts to strip blessings away from Jacob, God continuously came to Jacob's rescue. God provided and provided abundantly. Jacob's blessings kept multiplying, and God delivered on his promise to bless Jacob despite deception, manipulation, and abuse. The irony in the story implies that God sanctioned the result of Jacob's deception, the blessing, but God did not sanction Jacob's hands-on methods in accomplishing the blessing, the deception itself. Jacob not only deceived his father; he also took advantage of his father's weakness—an action not in alignment with God's heart.

Second Samuel 4 introduces readers to Mephibosheth. When the news of Saul and Jonathan's deaths reached home, Jonathan's son and his nurse fled from the Philistines. An accident occurred and crippled five-year-old Mephibosheth. He suffered an injury impacting his mobility (2 Sam. 4:4). He would never again run as swiftly or cover great distances. Time passed, and once David subdued the Philistines, the new king asked if anyone remained who belonged to Saul's family (2 Sam. 8:1; 9:1). Ziba, a servant of Saul's house, informed David that one of Jonathan's sons survived, and Mephibosheth came and fell at David's feet (2 Sam. 9:3, 6).

Kings of the ancient Near East regularly slaughtered rival claimants to the throne, but David, despite having been hounded by Saul for years, remained faithful to his oath to Jonathan and displayed tender kindness to the grandson of God's first-anointed king (2 Sam. 9:7–13). David restored to Mephibosheth all that had belonged to Saul, including Saul's fields, and he provided servants to tend those fields (2 Sam. 9:7, 10). David displayed warmth and honor toward Mephibosheth. The king treated him like a son, inviting Mephibosheth to eat at the king's table, a spot reserved for family members and dignitaries. The king also provided Mephibosheth with a house in Jerusalem. David's actions elevated Mephibosheth to an exalted position, a member of the royal household. As such, Mephibosheth's disability does not appear to have concerned David in the slightest.

When David fled from Absalom, Ziba took advantage of Mephibosheth's situation and lied to David. While delivering supplies to the on-the-run king, Ziba claimed that Mephibosheth hoped to use Absalom's rebellion to his advantage and reclaim the throne for Saul's household. David believed Ziba's lies and transferred all that belonged to Mephibosheth to the faithful Ziba (2 Sam. 16:1–4). When David returned to Jerusalem after Absalom's death in 2 Samuel 19, Mephibosheth rode a donkey to meet the king, a needed aid considering his mobility. Mephibosheth arrived before David, and his appearance, unwashed and unshaven, attested to the state of mourning Mephibosheth had maintained during the king's absence. When David asked why Mephibosheth did not go out with the king, fleeing with the rest of the king's faithful followers from Jerusalem, Mephibosheth shared that his disability had kept him from following the king, but that he had remained faithful to David.

When he heard Mephibosheth's side of the story, David divided the fields originally belonging to Saul between Ziba and Mephibosheth. The text does not inform readers why David divided the fields, who David believed, or how this event impacted Mephibosheth's status before the king. Regardless of David's response, Mephibosheth's own response to David's return remains beautiful. Mephibosheth did not care if Ziba got all the land. He trusted the king's judgment and rejoiced at the king's return.

Another notable person who struggled with a disability in the Old Testament includes Moses. When God appeared to Moses at the burning bush, Moses stated his public speaking lacked elegance; he admitted he struggled with a slowness of speech and tongue, implying a stutter. The Lord responded to Moses, saying, "Who has made man's mouth? Who makes him mute, or deaf, or seeing, or blind? Is it not I, the LORD?" (Exod. 4:10–11). God's statement that he made people who face disabilities of speech, hearing, and sight supports the conclusion Moses struggled with a stutter that fell into the category of a physical disability. It can also be inferred through God's statement that disability serves a purpose in God's plan; that a person does not become disabled out of sheer, random coincidence; and that, therefore, God still utilizes people with disabilities in mighty ways.

Moses continued to protest, and eventually God assigned Aaron to speak for Moses (Exod. 4:13–16). If Moses had stopped resisting God's plan to use him as his direct mouthpiece, Moses would have served as the direct connection between God and Pharaoh. Instead, Moses wound up providing Aaron with God's words to speak before Pharaoh and the people. Had Moses cooperated and allowed the Lord to use him in his area of weakness, Moses would have served as an example of God's ability to show his power made perfect in weakness, demonstrating within the Old Testament the idea found in the New Testament in 2 Corinthians 12:9. In fact, God weaves this very concept throughout the entire biblical record.

There are several implications of God asserting he himself has made the mute, the blind, and the deaf. One is that even though Moses had some sort of speech impediment, God chose him to do that which he would be the weakest at doing, humanly speaking. God receives more honor and glory in the face of weakness. The second implication of this account is that PWDs are not mistakes but are perfectly planned aspects of God's eternal plan. Disability is temporary, and we are moving to a state of completeness, restoration, or *shalom*. The existence of people with disabilities is not a hindrance to God's plan, but rather an advancement of it.

In fact, in one case, my (Jason's) disability gave me an opportunity to clearly present the gospel. At the time, I had previously spent eight weeks in a rehab hospital because of a medical mishap. That led to me developing a friendship with one of the head chaplains at the hospital. She and I met and talked, and she volunteered herself to serve as scribe for some of my Greek assignments. This was the one class I was able to keep that particular semester, primarily because of the sacrificial efforts of my Greek professor, Dr. Sauer, who regularly visited the hospital to tutor me. The friendship with this chaplain at the hospital led to an opportunity to start a Bible study. For my first year running the Bible study, no one showed, and I was discouraged, wondering if I was doing what God desired. However, in my next and final year, people started attending, one of whom asked me directly how he could be saved. Suffice it to say, I was in a moment of shock, never expecting such a direct request. However, I gave a quick gospel presentation, and he accepted Christ as his Savior. This turn of events was caused not only by my having a disability, but even by experiencing an unplanned medical mishap. And this simple illustration is just one small example of what I know to be true. Who knows what other ways God might have used me or others to lead people to himself? Indeed, God works in mysterious ways. No obstacle or disability is ever too great for God to accomplish his purposes!

Over and over, God uses the weak to shame the strong. He used a woman, Jael, instead of the warrior Barak, to bring down a big-shot general, Sisera (Judges 4–5). He chose Gideon, a guy too terrified to thresh wheat on a hill. He entrusted the hands of a shepherd, David, with his people rather than the hands of a tall, handsome guy, Saul

(1 Samuel 24). Jesus called a bunch of fishermen, not teachers, to start the church (Matthew 4). Weakness shows that the surpassing power appearing throughout these stories, and even our stories today, clearly belongs to God. Human weakness often allows God to reveal his power (2 Cor. 4:7–10). Remember, when we are weak, he is strong!

Moses missed his opportunity to allow God's strength to shine through his struggles. While God does utilize people with disabilities for his plan and their own good, the Old Testament implies disabilities result from the fallenness that plagues humanity. This is seen most poignantly in Genesis 3, where it is decreed that sin will affect all spheres of life: natural, male, and female. Paul's statement in Romans that creation groans for the sons of God to be revealed strengthens this implication. "For we know that the whole creation groans and suffers the pains of childbirth together until now. And not only that, but also we ourselves, having the first fruits of the Spirit, even we ourselves groan within ourselves, waiting eagerly for our adoption as sons and daughters, the redemption of our body" (Rom. 8:22–23 NASB).

"Stuttering": Mike's Story

"Please, Lord, take away my stutter. I can serve you so much better without it." I have prayed for this countless times in my life. You see, I have stuttered for about twenty years. Weirdly, my speech impediment did not start when I first began speaking but several years later. No one has been able to explain why. More than a decade of speech therapy gave me different speech tools but did not cure my stutter. Many people have also told me about various stutter cures that are fads or outright scams. As I approach thirty, I have accepted that, without a divine miracle, my stutter will always be a part of my life.

Over the last nine years, I have earned two degrees in historical theology from prominent evangelical institutions of higher education and completed two internships from well-known churches. Still, I am looking for a consistent role in ministry. Many churches are flummoxed with how to utilize my unique gifts. How do you use somebody with outstanding theological and historical training but who can't get through a sentence without blocking and stuttering? Most roles in ministry are speaking-based, from the pastor to the greeters. Small groups and Bible studies are speaking-based. Sunday school classes and evangelism are speaking-based. Administrative assistants and worship leaders are speaking-based. Counseling and leading prayers are speaking-based. How can you utilize the gifts of somebody in the church who struggles to speak fluently and sometimes can't speak at all for many seconds? I have yet to meet someone who can answer this question.

Going to seminary gave training in public speaking (preaching, leading prayer, learning how to counsel, leading Bible studies, teaching Sunday school classes, and teaching theology to lay believers). I got through the program by publicly speaking only when necessary, such as when preaching or giving different presentations. Both of my internships have been writing-based, which may be the area where I can help the church.

However, few churches have full-time writing positions. Most writing in churches, from devotionals to articles on a church's website, is handled by a pastor on staff who also has many speaking roles. In my life, I have realized most churches, when hiring interns or other employees, usually opt for the candidate who does not stutter over the one who does if all else is close to equal. As I have outlined, I understand why, as the vast majority of ministry is speaking-based. Still, I have asked many people at different churches, how can I pursue a career in vocational ministry when I have a severe speech impediment? I have more training than most Christians in the world. What I need is the right opportunity to serve. The Lord has not answered my prayer to remove my stutter. The reason will be revealed more clearly in the future. Until then, how can I serve the church when every role relies on fluent speech?

While on the one side we have the curse, on the other we have God often intervening directly, limiting the effects of sin. When the Israelites wandered in the wilderness, their clothes and shoes did not wear out (Deut. 29:5). Deuteronomy also shows this care at the close of Moses's life, when the book states that Moses's eyes did not wear out (Deut. 34:7). Both elements communicate God was miraculously protecting and preserving the people. God miraculously preserved Moses's functionality, keeping him from failing sight despite old age. Without God's assistance, Moses's eyes would have faded and the people would have been continually afflicted. This serves as a quasi-foretaste into the experiences we will have in both the millennial kingdom and the eternal state—living apart from sin.

In the meantime, the Old Testament offers to us a positive example of a person with a disability, an asset, and the person who befriends them, a handler. The widows Naomi and Ruth showcase what it looks like for those of their social status and physical abilities to fully seek out security. The text only shows Ruth gleaning. Scholars speculate that due to Naomi's age she was perhaps unable to glean. Other scholars believe that, due to Naomi's previously held wealthy status derived from a family of means, gleaning the fields would have been viewed as an act well beneath her status. If gleaning had been a viable option, it seems the two women would have gone out to glean the fields together. Regardless, Naomi's inability to glean lends greater weight to Ruth's commitment to stay with her mother-in-law (Ruth 1:16). Ruth may have recognized Naomi's inability to glean or to glean enough to sustain herself and, therefore, knew that Naomi desperately needed someone to meet her physical needs as well as someone to be her companion. Naomi's need compelled Ruth to make the ultimate sacrifice. Ruth left her country, her people, and her gods to seek her mother-in-law's God and the security he might provide.

Naomi's initial response to Ruth and Orpah's comments pushed the girls away. Her reply to her daughters-in-law might demonstrate Naomi's low self-esteem. She did not want to be a burden on anyone else. This often proves to be a relatable feeling for a person with a physical or mental disability. One of the main reasons we isolate ourselves is tied to our fear that if we involve ourselves with others, we might create too much trouble for them. We worry that our output will fall short of the required input we need to function alongside others. However, Ruth's story reminds us that hidden blessings exist for those who serve the disabled. Ruth selflessly seeks security for Naomi, and then God provides security for both of them. God rewards Ruth's sacrifice. The line of Jesse arrives through Ruth and Boaz, the line that leads to the birth of David and, by extension, of Jesus the Messiah, the Great Healer of all disabilities.

Ruth's selfless action that served to achieve Naomi's security speaks to Ruth's worthy character and her correct assumption that YHWH would provide and protect. Regardless of Naomi's disability status, Ruth shows readers an example of someone who serves another person who has been overlooked and marginalized. We see throughout Ruth's story that Ruth remains concerned with Naomi's well-being above her own. The book of Ruth portrays a mutual relationship where Ruth physically aids Naomi while Naomi shares her wisdom with Ruth, advising the young widow as she navigates a new culture. Naomi also does her best through her insights to usher Ruth into a new and secure life. Ruth and Naomi view one another as genuine friends. And genuine friendship serves as the ultimate purpose behind the Five-Step Plan which strives to foster equal partnership in the relationships it creates.

Chapter 5

DISABILITY IN THE NEW TESTAMENT

As a homeowner, I (Paul) am fascinated by the concept of curb appeal. Real estate experts tell us that by exerting just a bit more effort—polishing up our front yard or replacing our tired front door with a door with more pop—we can drastically increase our home's resale value. It amazes me how spending a relatively small amount of money on appearances brings such large financial gains when it comes time to sell a house.

I guess it is a little like selling a used car. How many of us normalize driving around town in a dirty car with a shabby interior, but when the time to sell or trade arrives, we scrub, wax, and buff our way to a like-new model. Appearance matters!

However, appearance alone is not as important as the substantive parts of our houses or cars, such as foundations and engines. A manicured front yard or popping door might catch people's attention and draw them into an open house. The intelligent investor, on the other hand, waits to read the inspection report on the house's foundation. The savvy used-car buyer is never impressed by a shiny new paint job. Veteran car folks wait for the results of the engine's compression test before making an offer to buy.

The same is not always true inside the body of Christ. Sometimes, the refurbished exteriors, clean and eye-catching, not only grab but maintain our attention. Believers may often view the shiny, outward appearance but fail to spend much time evaluating whether important parts are missing. In our research, we discovered many people with disabilities *want* to get involved and *attempt* to get involved with their local faith community only to discover pathways are blocked both literally and figuratively.

Allow me to reiterate the story of a specific discussion with my cowriter and former student, Jason Epps. I (Paul) knew from our preaching class that Jason struggled with cerebral palsy. I was well aware Jason was confined to a power wheelchair. But I could not answer his simple question of whether I believed upon graduation he could find a church that might wish to hire him as their pastor. What were my misgivings? I did not want to provide Jason with a false hope that there would be a *normal* number of ministry openings coming his way.

There is no such thing as a perfect ministerial candidate, just as there are no perfect churches. All pastoral candidates possess flaws. Many of these are painted over during the interview or vetting process. But for most candidates with disabilities, the flaws lie out in the open, on display for all to see. This is where the ugly bias creeps into the hiring process. Most congregations would prefer to hire a *model* minister, whatever that happens to be for that community: married rather than single; two children rather than none; a stay-at-home spouse rather than one serving in the workforce; or an incredible communicator who demonstrates charisma, humor, and witty wisdom rather than a boring sermonizer.

I have become convinced one of the main reasons we disregard or overlook people in our midst with disabilities owes to a misinterpretation of 1 Corinthians 6:15–20.[1] In that passage, Paul uses the metaphor of the temple of God to demonstrate why unity and purity are essential within the body of Christ.

---

1. Nicholas G. Piotrowski and Ryan Johnson, "One Spirit, One Body, One Temple: Paul's Corporate Temple Language in 1 Corinthians 6," *Journal of the Evangelical Theological Society* 65, no. 4 (2022): 733–52.

Instead of believing the Jewish notion that Christians *collectively* make up the temple, we adopt the idea that each of our own, individual bodies serves as a unique temple of God. And we want this individualized temple to look good. We want our unique temples to function well and look good for ourselves, for others, and even for God. In addition, we want our privatized, isolated temple to look good to lost people. We long to offer curb appeal to people who are outside of the church and, sometimes, we will do whatever it takes to make our local congregation pop for the unsaved passerby.

We reveal our private priorities, worrying and asking questions like: "What if we have visitors in here on a Sunday morning while we are *platforming* one of our members with intellectual or developmental disabilities? What if they don't come back after they witness someone like *that* leading our congregation in worship?" We secretly fear God cannot use some of his children, that it is impossible for God to use certain individuals due to their disabilities. However, God's Word makes it clear he delights to use the least expected family members to work wonders. Early on in Moses's career, he was hesitant to fulfill the call to speak on behalf of God to Pharaoh and to the Israelites because of his speech. Therefore, God allowed him the use of Aaron as a spokesperson. However, in Deuteronomy, we see Moses speaking directly on behalf of God. His confidence has increased, and he serves in the role of God's original call. Indirectly, Moses's need of confidence is very much aligned with the principles of the Five-Step Plan in overcoming baggage (Deut. 1, 5). Moses himself, in the context of Exodus 4, is dealing with the baggage of rejection when he tried to intervene in the confrontation of the two Israelite brothers (Exod. 2).

In addition, we often adopt the samsara paradigm which crept into the disciples' thinking.[2] When the disciples encountered a man born blind (not on account of an accident or a disease), the disciples guessed the blind man must have done something wrong, and they asked Jesus who had committed the sin, the blind man or his parents. Jesus answered, "It was not that this man sinned, or his parents, but that the works of God might be displayed in him" (John 9:3).

---

2. Robin Hadaway, *A Survey of World Missions*, Kindle edition (Nashville: B&H Publishing Group, 2020), 118.

By judging our friends with disabilities on outward appearance alone, we grossly underestimate the work and witness God wants to accomplish in and through them. Why do we care if someone takes a bit longer than normal to make an announcement from a sanctuary stage? Because it makes us feel uncomfortable. Is that a good enough reason not to invite our brothers and sisters with disabilities to make announcements? Why are we in a hurry to move through a worship service? Because in our fast-paced, technologically driven culture, stillness is awkward and un-comfortable. Is that a good enough reason to prohibit those who might hinder the speed of the service from sharing? God might be using our brother or sister who moves more slowly to invite the rest of us into a slower space where it is easier to hear from him or worship him.

The New Testament presents a revolutionary perspective on people with disabilities. Instead of emphasizing their sins or their lack of "curb appeal," Jesus and his church emphasize the faith, determination, and hope belonging to people with disabilities.

"A Gift to the Church": Clair's Story

I was twenty-three. It was an average Sunday, nothing special. I drove into the parking lot, excited to hear God's Word, worship with friends, and enjoy their fellowship. Walking into the sanctuary, I headed to my regular seat, wanting to be right near the worship band. I loved to sing. Singing made my heart feel so close to Jesus. The service began, worship as usual. My heart? At rest. Then, like a splash of icy water on my face, the sermon began. The topic? Healing the disabled. My pastor said things like, "God wants you to be healed. If you only believe. Cancer, high blood pressure, depression . . . just ask, and you shall receive healing." My heart stopped. It was happening. Again. I had been diagnosed with type 1 diabetes at fourteen years old. My disability has no known cause. My disability has no cure. I use an insulin pump to deliver life-saving insulin. I have scars all over my body from where I've injected myself. I can't count how many times I've almost died. I had to give up career dreams, friends, and my childhood.

At fourteen years old, my world changed forever. I was at death's door, living out the nightmare of having to figure out how to be my own pancreas. Depression and anxiety diagnoses followed. Type 1 diabetes robbed me of so much joy in this life. And then my pastor said, "Have you asked him to heal you?" Everything inside me wanted to scream, *I've been asking Him to heal me since day one! It's me! I'm the problem! If my pastor says that all I have to do is ask and I've done that, then maybe God doesn't want to heal me. I don't deserve to be healed.*

Those thoughts lived with me well into my late twenties. I still love my former pastor. I still respect him. And I still think he's doing remarkable things in God's name. But his message that God heals people with disabilities if only they ask has haunted me for years. That message made me feel unloved. Unworthy. Like maybe God gave me this disease to punish me. That message minimized the intimacy I shared with Christ through his suffering and mine.

Years later, attending a counseling session, I told my therapist, "I feel like I'm a burden to the world. I feel like my disability disqualifies me from serving the church. I feel like he broke me on purpose. God must not love me. I've asked for healing. But it never comes." I will never forget what she said to me. It changed me forever. She said, "You are a gift to the church. You are the living example of carrying your cross daily. The church should be coming alongside you and supporting you in your disability, seeking to learn from you, especially learning how it's possible to be hopeful even during suffering. You are a gift, not a disqualified servant."

From that day forward, I challenged the leadership. I even told family and friends that my suffering shows a living embodiment of hope. If someone like me can believe God is still good, then you can too. This story is just one example of many times in my life when people have tried to "heal" me. I have experienced this in churches and my seminary and friend groups. It's heartbreaking. The disability community displays living proof that hope can live in the darkest of places.

The great prophet and emancipator Moses claimed a disability, somewhat shockingly, in response to his Maker's call on his life. When YHWH told his servant Moses that he would speak on God's behalf before Pharaoh, Moses protested, pointing to his own lack of eloquence, begging, "Oh, my Lord, I am not eloquent, either in the past or since you have spoken to your servant, but I am slow of speech and of tongue" (Exod. 4:10).

We often think of Moses and his speech problem when we think of disabilities in the Old Testament. It is almost comical that God would choose someone with a speech disability to serve as his spokesperson. At the very least, it is ironic. However, the apostle Paul wrote, "But God chose what is foolish in the world to shame the wise; God chose what is weak in the world to shame the strong" (1 Cor. 1:27). And if Moses is the patron saint of speech pathology in the Old Testament, surely the apostle Peter is the epitome of ADHD in the New Testament.

Anyone who suffers from ADHD in all its various and nefarious forms can spot this malady in Peter from a mile away. Frequently he opens his mouth only to insert his foot. It is true Peter gave insightful testimony that the carpenter from Nazareth was the long-awaited Messiah. And it is true Jesus chose Peter to help start the church. However, aside from Peter's testimony and the fact Jesus *did* choose Peter to usher the church into her earliest days, Peter does not seem like the kind of ideal choice for a leadership position inside a budding congregation, much less an entire faith family.

We also know Peter suffered from a debilitating disease: people-pleasing, an all-too-common malady. When he was with the Jewish leaders who had converted to The Way, Peter abided by the kosher dietary restrictions. But when he was dining with the new Gentile converts, he enjoyed the full menu, pork chops included (Gal. 2:12–13). Friends in the Galatian church must have experienced severe whiplash trying to keep up with Peter's rotating dinner guests and his vacillating dining habits.

Words describing Peter include *talkative*, *brash*, and *impulsive*. The other disciples might have considered nicknames like "Rambler" or "Hot Head" as appropriate titles for their somewhat reckless comrade. "Solid Rock" seems like a stretch, but that is the moniker Jesus gave Peter. When Peter saw Jesus, in all his *shekinah* glory, along with Moses and Elijah, Peter blurted out something about wanting to build booths on the spot to set up a kind of commercial tourist attraction (Mark 9:5). Perhaps only our Lord could see the strong and stable *rocky* deep inside the *flighty*

Peter, who would deny even *knowing* the Nazarene when a young girl confronted him (Mark 14:71).

If a church today were forming a leadership committee, no doubt Peter's nomination to serve would fail for lack of a second. You can almost hear the whispers. "Peter? I don't know. From what I understand, he suffers from ADHD. Do we really want someone like *that* on our important committee?"

As readers of the New Testament, we are let in on the positive aspects of Peter's leadership qualities. These are positive leadership aspects we might deny people with disabilities the opportunity to exhibit by not involving them in leadership. Apparently, when Jesus approached his disciples, walking toward them on the water in the middle of a storm, all the other disciples sat in silence while Peter spoke up and asked if he could join Jesus out on the water (Matt. 14:22–33). Yes, Peter often blurted out meaningless speeches, but you must admit, he was also the only one with enough faith and courage to walk on the water with Jesus, even if it did not last long. Peter's story shows his flaws *and* his strengths.

What we are emphasizing in this book is this truth: *do not overlook the incredible gifts possessed by the friends with disabilities who fill your life.* Instead of always placing a guy like Peter in the fixed category of *dreamer* or *airhead,* consider seeing him as our Savior saw him. Jesus saw a man who exhibited incredible faith and a clear vision of who he believed Jesus to be—the Christ, the Son of God (Matt. 16:16). Do you see your friends with disabilities as gifted people with incredible faith and possessing a clear vision of who Jesus is?

JESUS AND MIRACLES

We see many instances of Jesus's healing ministry in the New Testament. Even the summary statements which describe his itinerant ministry mention the many miracles Jesus accomplished. Jesus was going about in all of Galilee, "teaching in their synagogues and proclaiming the gospel of the kingdom and healing every disease and every affliction among the people" (Matt. 4:23).

The writer of Hebrews informs us, "Jesus Christ is the same yesterday and today and forever" (Heb. 13:8). However, many today wonder whether

Jesus still heals people with disabilities. There are two schools of thought on this topic. One is labeled "cessationism" and the other "continuationism." Broadly, cessationism argues that speaking in tongues, prophecy, and healing are no longer normative gifts for the church but were limited to the early church to affirm its validity. God can and still does perform miracles, but those gifts of the Spirit are no longer exercised in the same way that teaching, mercy, and shepherding are. Continuationism, however, argues that all spiritual gifts still function in the church today, just as in the early church. Thus, all spiritual gifts, including healing, are given to believers today. Within each camp, a broad spectrum of belief exists. However, for the purposes here, the question of whether individuals in the church could be given the gift of healing is the most relevant.

Amy Kenny, a refreshing and witty scholar with a disability, notes, "The assumption that disability needs 'fixing' is dehumanizing."[3] In her book, *My Body Is Not a Prayer Request: Disability Justice in the Church*, she describes those who think all people with disabilities should be healed as those who try to *pray away the cane*. The assumption underlying this belief is that disability is uniquely wrong and in need of fixing. Gluttony (a vice) need not be prayed away, but a limp (a physical reality) must be. This is all wrong, she writes, saying that "disability unveils God's work to the community, if only people are willing to receive it."[4]

Her book includes several top ten lists. One of the most startling lists is a list from the least jarring to the most shocking of unsolicited disability theologies (also called unhelpful, unsolicited advice) that folks have shared with her.

10. Jesus wants to see you running.
9. If you just believed, God would heal you.
8. What sin in your life is preventing you from getting up and walking?
7. Adam and Eve weren't disabled, so that's not God's plan for humanity.

---

3.   Amy Kenny, *My Body Is Not a Prayer Request: Disability Justice in the Church* (Grand Rapids: Brazos Press, 2022), 4.
4.   Kenny, *My Body Is Not a Prayer Request*, 7.

6. You need to hope for more from life than disability.
5. There are no wheelchairs in heaven.
4. Everything happens for a reason.
3. Jesus didn't die for you to be in a wheelchair.
2. God doesn't give us more than we can handle, so you must be able to handle this!
1. God doesn't see you as disabled.[5]

Can you imagine the hurt and pain these kinds of statements cause for our brothers and sisters with disabilities? Regardless of their motivation, they betray a theology that holds there should be no car accidents, tornadoes, or bad colds. Yes, Jesus performed miracles of healing because of his incredible love and compassion, and to validate his claims of messianic authority.

His healings were miracles. They were not the norm. His miracles served as divine interruptions (reversals) of common maladies. They were instances in time when heaven touched this fallen earth in the most visceral ways. The miracles of Jesus show his ultimate authority in and over a broken land. His simple spoken word or touch proved to be enough to reverse the curse in special, temporary circumstances. These events were unusual—out of the ordinary. To believe that all persons with disabilities can or should be healed reduces them to objects of pity. *It is a shame all those with disabilities cannot be normal like us.* This thinking betrays an incorrect definition of *normal*.

One of the phrases in the disability literature that jumped out at us was the term *temporarily able-bodied.* At first, we were confused by it. But the more we pondered its meaning, the more convinced we became of its profundity. After all, are not each of us so-called "able-bodied" people one accident, one stroke, or one brain injury away from being disabled? And in the end, when each of us, by God's common grace, reaches old age (whatever that is) and our bodies begin to naturally break down and that breakdown causes pain, will we not then be *disabled* to varying degrees?

So, to get out of the binary way of thinking that we are *either* disabled or able-bodied, it seems refreshing to re-name the two categories

---

5. Kenny, *My Body Is Not a Prayer Request*, 172.

disabled or *temporarily able-bodied*. Thinking of ourselves as temporarily able-bodied brings with it a certain sense of humility we may otherwise lack, a reminder of our fragile condition and our ever-present closeness to the reality of disabilities. We look down our noses at the disabled or view them with patronizing pity until we realize that we also—yes, you, dear reader—will one day be disabled to some degree.

This seems to be Jesus's focus when he interacted with the people who had disabilities. The people he healed were not given eternal, glorified bodies. They were healed in a temporary sense only to later die. This is to say the healthy human body is not a sign of special divine blessing, or that a person with a disability is less than human and existing under some type of divine curse. How easily we fall into the same trap the disciples slid into when they asked, "Who sinned, the blind man or his parents?" We default to a worldview that incorrectly embraces such ideas as:

- *I am normal and healthy. Therefore, God is good.*
- *She has an awful disability. A good God wouldn't allow this.*

No! The correct view is

- *There are people with disabilities and people who are temporarily able-bodied. And God is good.*
- *There are people with disabilities and people who are temporarily able-bodied. And both are living lives touched by the fall and its results.*

Jesus's ministry of miracles and healing provided a brief glimpse into a forthcoming, eternal state in the newly constituted or renewed earth. Jesus's actions were *coming attractions*, a preview of things to come. His physical miracles of healing were like the hors d'oeuvres for a long-awaited, future dinner party. The apostle Paul reminded the Philippians of this truth when he penned, "But our citizenship is in heaven, and from it we await a Savior, the Lord Jesus Christ, who will transform our lowly body to be like his glorious body, by the power that enables him even to subject all things to himself" (Phil. 3:20–21).

When Christ returns to dwell on the earth, believers will receive resurrection bodies (Rom. 6:5; 8:11). Jesus will resurrect those believers who have died, and they will receive bodies matching their Savior's resurrected body, perfect and incorruptible. Christ will also transform believers still living on earth so that their mortal bodies will also reflect his resurrection body (1 Thess. 4:13–18). Those glorified bodies will never experience pain or sorrow. Jesus will wash away the fall and all its residue. In an instant, Christ's appearance will forever banish death's sting and brush away all tears (1 Cor. 15:51–56; Rev. 21:4). Christ will make all things new.

This truth personally serves as a great relief. In the eternal state, I (Jason) will not be bound by my physical limitations. I will be able to run into God's throne room and get on my knees and worship. I have always felt an immense longing to worship God on my knees. This especially becomes poignant when worshippers in a church service are asked to get on their knees. I have never felt I was excluded or isolated from that invitation because every time they have asked, they have always mentioned, "if you are willing and able." But I always long to kneel. (Coincidentally, I also look forward to hunting down all the guys from my college-dorm floor and wrestling with them for hours on end to get back at them for all the wrestling and screaming they did when I was trying to sleep at two o'clock in the morning!)

What I really look forward to is no longer being excluded from activities, but being able to do anything anyone else is doing without having to think of potential workarounds. I look forward to that kind of freedom. Whether it is freedom to participate in sports or to do whatever else the activity might be with a large group of people, currently in this life there is always something that prevents me, some aspect of the activity I cannot do with the rest of the group so that I physically cannot participate. It bothers me I cannot join in. I want to experience the sense that there are no barriers to community. Even in the best possible situation here on earth, there is always going to be some sort of barrier.

Our future remains secure. God will dwell with humanity and make all things new. That glorious future serves as a reminder that God longs to redeem his people. God's redemption includes the restoration of his people's physical bodies, including the bodies of his people with disabilities. Christ waits on the Father to tell him when to begin the holy re-creation of the current fallen creation. He looks forward to that day when he makes all things new, and so do his people (Matt. 24:36; 26:29). Throughout his earthly ministry, Jesus healed people with all sorts of disabilities, including the blind, the lame, the crippled, and the mute (Matt. 15:30–31; 21:14). Those healings provided little glimpses into Christ's coming kingdom when Christ will heal all disabilities.

That future hope also serves as a reminder that our limitations do not form the core of our identities. Our identities are not rooted in our abilities or disabilities. Believers have been united to Christ, and our identities are rooted in him (Eph. 2:11–22). Things like athleticism, hearing, and memory fade over time, but our bond with Christ never fades. It always remains, crafted and maintained by the Lord who conquered death, claiming the victory over the fall and all its consequences.

While we know God desires for his people to be good stewards of their bodies, God also places a heavier emphasis on sanctification over physical conditioning (1 Tim. 4:7–10). The apostle Paul notes our difficulties in life are accomplishing an eternal glory, and these trials and troubles of life are only momentary and fleeting. He writes,

> So we do not lose heart. Though our outer self is wasting away, our inner self is being renewed day by day. For this light momentary affliction is preparing for us an eternal weight of glory beyond all comparison, as we look not to the things that are seen but to the things that are unseen. For the things that are seen are transient, but the things that are unseen are eternal. (2 Cor. 4:16–18)

When Christ brings those unseen things to bear throughout creation, there will be no pain, sorrow, or physical limitations. He longs to make all things new. Christ will straighten out the things that tangle up and distort our identities. Already, he renews our inner self day by day, and one day, he will renew our entire self so we will be like him, clearly mirroring the one who stands at the core of our identities.

BARTIMAEUS: SON OF HONOR

Among counselors and social workers, the words "shame" and "guilt" function differently. Guilt is associated with an action. For example, if someone were to steal a bicycle, she would be guilty because of her action. However, shame is associated with identity. If someone were to chronically steal bicycles, he would be a thief. The thief would carry this negative title as part of his identity. Many with disabilities feel ashamed of their limitations. While limited mobility or impaired hearing is not a sin, many PWDs report feeling shame, isolation, and loneliness because of their disability.

In Mark 10:46–52 we read about a man named Bartimaeus. His name, using the Aramaic prefix meaning "son," is literally "son of Timaeus." Timaeus refers to the Greek word τιμή, which means "honor." Bartimaeus is then the "son of honor." The name conjures up images of Boaz, calling and blessing those in his fields. This Bartimaeus may be like David, a fierce warrior with steadfast devotion to the Lord.

Yet, when readers meet Bartimaeus, they find no person of honor. Instead, the blind man sits at the city gate, begging for his daily needs. The "son of honor" knows no honor in the sandy city of Jericho—he will never be seated at the head of any tables or thanked by city magistrates for his contribution to the flourishing of the city. He sits at the gate, moving his mat during the day to avoid the relentless sun. He is a pitiful sight, more aptly called *Bar-Boosh*, the "son of shame."

Shame expert Brené Brown, however, argues vulnerability is not weakness. Brown says, "Vulnerability is our most accurate measurement of courage—to be vulnerable, to let ourselves be seen, to be honest."[6] Bartimaeus must have struggled with shame. But for one moment, his special moment, he pushed all of that aside and cried out to Jesus the Nazarene. Bartimaeus acted with courage to rival that of Boaz and David—a courage born not from ability, but vulnerability.

In this story, Jesus was traveling toward Jerusalem with his esteemed entourage. They were walking purposely. They were on a mission. Jericho

---

6. Brene Brown, "Listening to Shame," *TED Talk*, accessed on August 16, 2022, www.singjupost.com/brene-brown-on-listening-to-shame-at-ted-talk-full-transcript/?s-inglepage=1.

sits at the bottom of the Jordan Rift Valley, which left Jesus fourteen miles and more than three thousand feet of ascent of travel to Jerusalem, where he would soon take his last earthly breath.

The disciples were unaware of that end; they strode alongside Christ, eager for honor and prestige. In fact, the verses just prior to Bartimaeus's arrival feature James's and John's hopeful request to sit at his right and left hands in glory. Jesus takes their statement and offers a radical reframing. He came to serve, not to be served. His kingdom would honor the servants and slaves, not those who asked him first.

Bartimaeus, unaware of this conversation, had faith in Jesus from Nazareth, the Son of David, the Messiah. In his most vulnerable moment, the blind beggar shouted over the din, "Jesus, Son of David, have mercy on me!" Bartimaeus's use of this special name shows his insight into Jesus's identity as the Messiah. Bartimaeus shoved past his fear and worked up the courage to get past the uncomfortable.

Surely the crowds were impressed with Bartimaeus's insight into seeing Jesus the Nazarene for who he really was. The crowds must have been amazed that Bartimaeus, an unskilled, blind beggar, saw Jesus more accurately than even the disciples who had been with Jesus for three years. Or maybe not.

Unfortunately, that was *not* how the crowd or even the disciples reacted to Bartimaeus's moment of vulnerability. Instead, they scolded him like an unruly kindergartener. Mark relays, "Many rebuked him, telling him to be silent." This is a polite way of saying the crowd began *shaming* Bartimaeus. It was hot and sandy; the last thing they needed was an obnoxious and shameful beggar interrupting the Messiah's march.

We can imagine the insults. "What a loser! Does he think he can join *our* elite group and walk with Jesus toward his inauguration and installation as king?" They probably yelled, "Shut up, you no good beggar. What would you know about theological issues? We are the ones who have followed Jesus around. The learned ones. Sit there and be quiet. You need to know your place in this world!" Even though his name meant "son of honor," those Jesus followers were certainly not holding back the shame they poured out onto Bartimaeus. Until their leader, Jesus the Nazarene, called for the blind beggar. Then, in a moment of extreme humility, Jesus stopped. *God* stopped. God-in-flesh paused in the heat and sand, and he recognized this blind man for who he was. This was not a blind beggar or an unruly child. No, this was *Bartimaeus*. This was one of his sons of honor. In his bestseller *Gentle and Lowly: The Heart of Christ for Sinners and Sufferers*, Dane Ortlund observes, "The deeper into weakness and suffering and testing we go, the deeper Christ's solidarity with us. As we go down into pain and anguish, we are descending ever deeper into Christ's very heart, not away from it."[7] The traveling party, including the disciples, wanted to pass by Bartimaeus. Better to keep on moving and avoid a potentially embarrassing or messy scene. Engaging with a blind beggar could be so uncomfortable. But Jesus, on his way to the cross, desired to stop—to ease another's suffering as he headed toward his own suffering.

In a humbling moment for the disciples, Jesus asked the same question of Bartimaeus that he had asked of James and John just a few hours prior—"What do you want me to do for you?" In that scenario, James and John asked for precedence. They desired prominence, to reign right beside Jesus. Bartimaeus answered the same question differently. The blind man blurted out an answer that I (Paul) believe any of us with disabilities might have shouted out in that precious moment: "Rabbi, let me recover my sight." In Greek, Bartimaeus's request is beautifully brief: Ραββουνι, ἵνα ἀναβλέψω ("Teacher, I want to see"). Bartimaeus could have asked for glory and honor like the disciples had. Yet he only asked to regain his sight. This verse reveals that Bartimaeus wasn't born blind, but rather that he had lost his sight later in life ("I want to see . . . again").

Bartimaeus's request shows a heart of faith. "I know I am not whole. Help me." Those with disabilities are not uniquely in need of redemption. No one can travel through life unscathed. Whether blinded in an accident, traumatized by childhood abuse, or simply scuffed by mundane sins, we all need to be made whole. Bartimaeus stands as a paradigm of faith, submitting his shame to the only One who can make him whole.

In Mark 10:52, Jesus responds that the blind man's faith has made him well or has saved him. The Greek term that Jesus uses to refer to the blind

---

7. Dane Ortlund, *Gentle and Lowly: The Heart of Christ for Sinners and Sufferers* (Wheaton, IL: Crossway, 2020), 57.

man's being healed or saved, σῴζω, carries the meaning of being cured, made whole, restored, or saved. Bartimaeus feels like he lacks something intrinsic. He believes that there is something not quite right with himself. Bartimaeus struggles with a continual feeling of being *lesser than*.

In my (Paul) struggles with non-hyperactive ADHD, I have often experienced the same feeling. It is more than simply feeling like I am always running late or always misplacing important items or continually missing key details such as, "Where in the invitation did it say we were supposed to dress in Western wear?" The uneasy emotion is more of wishing the non-hyperactive ADHD would just go away at least for a season, hoping that I could be just like other seminary students who remembered the names and dates of the many church fathers and what each believed; that I could pass Greek and Hebrew language quizzes without cramming all morning; or, perhaps, that I could recall with ease the many algebra formulas foisted upon me by well-meaning mathematics teachers. (I once asked my patient wife how one knows which *memorized* formula to use with which equation. She slowly responded, "You . . . just . . . remember." She might as well have said, "You just sprinkle the magic algebra dust!")

Like Brene Brown warned, I often eschew vulnerability for pride. I toss courage to the sidelines to fit in and feel, well, normal. After someone quotes a bit of early church history and mentions the Council of Orange, like we are all church history experts, I think to myself, *Oh, sure: The Councils of Orange? "Two church synods held in Orange, France, in 441 and 529. The first, under the presidency of St. Hilary of Arles, dealt mainly with disciplinary matters. The second, and by far the more important, was concerned with refuting the semi-Pelagianism of Faustus of Riez." Who doesn't know that?*[8]

The more times I engage with my friend and coauthor Jason Epps, the more impressed I am with his enthusiastic vulnerability. Of course, he has shared his feelings of loneliness and isolation. Sometimes he would rather stay at home, alone, than turn into a burden at a party or social event due to the accessibility struggles he faces with his powered chair. But overall, he is full steam ahead with his vision and his goal of seeing

---

8.   Councils of Orange, accessed February 15, 2024, https://www.britannica.com/topic/councils-of-Orange.

persons with a disability paired up with new friends who take a genuine interest in building authentic alliances. Building this type of spiritual friendship is truly doing the work of God in this broken world.

The call to remember the truth that faith in Jesus takes away all our shame may sound simplistic. "There is therefore now no condemnation for those who are in Christ Jesus" (Rom. 8:1). Further, that call might sound like pie in the sky, an invitation to remind ourselves that as Christians we will one day receive a new body, a perfected body. A body free of spastic cerebral palsy. A new body where the motor cortex in the brain works flawlessly. A brain free of non-hyperactive ADHD. But it is really an invitation to remind ourselves of what we currently have as Christians: a life with Jesus the Nazarene. A life free from shame and guilt. A life with Jesus, the Son of David, whose mercy makes all things new. We are asking you to do what Bartimaeus, the son of honor, did on that dusty road in Jericho. We are asking you to get past "uncomfortable." We are asking you to get engaged. Are you willing to trust God to help you build an authentic friendship with a person with a disability?

PAUL AND HIS THORN

We could probably fill a room with all the volumes that have been written on Paul and his mysterious illness (if it really was an illness and not an antagonistic enemy of the gospel). While the antagonist theory remains a possibility, most scholars believe Paul suffered from an ongoing physical malady. The absence of any mention of a specific medical diagnosis has led to endless speculations regarding Paul's condition. While we do not know precisely what the affliction was, we do know that Paul referred to his struggle as his thorn in the flesh (2 Cor. 12:7). Many commentators point to circumstantial evidence in the Scriptures showing Paul might have suffered with vision issues or watery eyes. Paul mentioned the oversized handwriting he used in writing to the Galatians (Gal. 6:11). Paul also said the Galatians would have plucked out their own eyes and given them to him if it would have been possible or brought Paul relief (Gal. 4:13–15). Some even suggest that his thorn may have been a chronic eye disease or a result from an injury he suffered when he was stoned in Lystra (Acts 14:19–20).

While speculating on the exact nature of Paul's opposition or thorn is interesting, we do not want to bury the lead. The main headline is that after earnest prayer for the removal of his thorn, God instead provided ongoing grace to survive the ordeal. Imagine! If the mighty apostle Paul was denied miraculous intervention, why do some people today *insist* that all should be healed? This is a form of modern-day materialism that only healthy, whole bodies are acceptable in the faith community.

There is an ugly theological worldview making the rounds. That distorted view states that God is willing and able to heal any who are injured and people with disabilities, but some of those with disabilities simply do not have enough faith to receive their healing. We can assume these same modern materialists would accuse even the apostle Paul of not having enough trust. Yes, there are miracles of healing in the New Testament. But they are not normative. They are *miracles*. And miracles seem to arise during the time frames of the three great epochs or eras of validation. Miracles in Scripture show up as signs to validate the law (Moses), the prophets (Elijah), and the launch of the church (Jesus). These three personages appear together at the miraculous Mount of Transfiguration.

In addition, to accuse a person with a disability of not having enough faith to believe in their healing adds insult to injury. As we discovered in so many of our interviews, most people with disabilities longed for a new body. But they also mentioned over and over how God had met so many of their needs. Many told of how their disability allowed them to closely identify with others around them who also lived with difficulties and deep needs. Would they wish their disability away? Of course! But as one husband told us regarding his wife who suffered for years with degenerative multiple sclerosis, "If God chose to miraculously heal my wife in an instant, I would give him all the praise. However, if I come home this afternoon and my wife is still lying in bed and smiles at me when I walk into the bedroom, I will *still* have enough faith to believe God has been good to our family."

In the next chapter, we will investigate what it might look like for you to engage, to push past the uncomfortable, to incorporate all people within the body of Christ into the daily life of the local church regardless of their status as a person with disabilities or a temporarily able-bodied person.

Chapter 6

PEWS TO PULPIT

The biblical vision for the church involves all people from all lands: male, female, young, old, with and without disabilities. We have discussed physical and social barriers to greater involvement on behalf of our brothers and sisters with disabilities, but the solution aims for full integration from the pews to the pulpits. In this chapter, we want to look at how churches can implement effective disability ministries, include those with disabilities in leadership positions, and conduct a disability audit to find solutions to problem areas in their own congregations.

EFFECTIVE DISABILITY MINISTRIES

In our research for this book, we were honored to interview child and adolescent psychiatrist Dr. Stephen Grcevich, who serves as founder and president of Key Ministry.[1] Grcevich sees several trends emerging related to upcoming growth in the disability ministry field. His predictions include:

---

1. Key Ministry, accessed June 23, 2023, www.keyministry.org. Key Ministry works to develop collaborations with church leaders, professionals, and organizations both within and outside the disability ministry movement.

- The church's care for vulnerable people will grow in importance as a strategy for gospel witness in a culture becoming increasingly hostile and skeptical to traditional Christianity.
- Disability ministry will be less "siloed"—less of a stand-alone ministry and more of a collaboration with all of the essential ministries within the church.
- Live disability ministry training will become much more available—through seminaries, churches and parachurch organizations.
- The terms "special needs ministry" and "inclusion ministry" will slowly fall out of use.
- Ministry in the 2020s will be characterized by an expanded focus on care and support of families impacted by disability.
- Disability inclusion in Christian schools will become much more common.[2]

Including people with disabilities is not only a moral responsibility; it also represents the heartbeat of Father God. God's heartbeat is *for* the suffering and brokenhearted. He sees and loves. In fact, God is love! John wrote, "So we have come to know and to believe the love that God has for us. God is love, and whoever abides in love abides in God, and God abides in him" (1 John 4:16).

True love involves action. The kingdom-of-God love, that Jesus kind of love, always includes serving others. This is the self-emptying form of love Jesus demonstrated throughout his life. Jesus always showed compassion toward those who had been marginalized, hurt, or pushed to the corners. In fact, the rare times when Jesus did wind up showing contempt or anger, he directed those emotions toward the self-righteous religious leaders of his day.

When we emphasize advocating for full participation from the pew to the pulpit we ask, "How is your church doing in ministering to the

---

2.   Stephen Grcevich, "Ten Disability Ministry Trends to Watch in the 2020s," Key Ministry, January 5, 2020, www.keyministry.org/church4everychild/2020/1/5/ten-disability-ministry-trends-to-watch-in-the-2020s.

disabled in your community?" Once this question has been tackled, the next question ought to be, "Of those disabled members of your fellowship, how actively involved are they in the life of your church?" Part of our continual cry to see persons with a disability as fully human involves seeing their potential for active, ongoing ministry involvement. The Scriptures make it no secret that all believers are called to active service in the body of Christ. We believe this also involves those who happen to struggle with a disability. One of the themes which emerged over and again in our research for this work was the idea of avoiding patronizing pity toward those with a disability. Does pity push PWDs in our churches to the active-ministry sidelines?

At my (Jason's) church, the people have a positive mindset toward PWDs. Whenever we have social events or outings, multiple people ask if I need help. In fact, one time when the church was being set up for a potluck, several people asked whether I would be able to maneuver and get through the tables. Most people only wonder about this potential obstacle after the tables have been set up.

In addition, there have been numerous occasions where I arrived late to men's Bible study and as soon as I got there, the men went out of their way to make a spot for me at one of the main tables. The first time something like this happened in Sunday school, it felt like the parable of the banquet because I tried to slink into the back, out of the way, but several of the leaders encouraged me to take up a position at one of the more central tables. Related to this, when I first found my current church, they apologized profusely that the men's restroom door was not automatic. They did not have the funds to make this modification, but they were already thinking about that *incorporation mindset.*

Several individuals in church (or their families) have some form of physical disability, which spurs on this positive mindset. The pastor's brother has cerebral palsy. This attitude seems to trickle down from the pastor to everyone else. This positive mindset really excited me. I decided to pursue leadership at the church, knowing that unlike other churches I had visited, this church would not give me a service position out of pity or offer me lip service, saying that they want me to serve without giving me anything to do.

When I began to fill out the paperwork to serve as a small group leader, it was clear that they would not accept me. However, it was not my disability that stopped them. Rather, the church and I disagreed on some secondary issues. Normally a rejection would hurt, but this time it was refreshing. I was finally being treated like everyone else.

That response would have been the same response the church would have given to someone who was not disabled. Most importantly, they would not give me the position out of pity. Despite not having a leadership position, I continue to have a great relationship with the head pastor, who has become one of my strongest cheerleaders in my doctoral program.

Often, able-bodied people in the church reason, "I don't want to bother them by asking them to serve. They are having a hard enough time just getting through their day!" But many PWDs would rather be asked to be involved or challenged to serve than be ignored. Our interviews revealed that PWDs with more fully developed mental capacities were sometimes asked to serve as a greeter or asked to distribute church bulletins because they sensed the church leader felt this was all they could do. An effective ministry with and for those with disabilities emphasizes friendship, challenges expectations, and explores individuality.

These stories serve to demonstrate necessary principles for effective disability ministry that will be further developed in the next section of the book. First, notice those with disabilities and the challenges they may be facing. Second, engage those with disabilities—ask how they're doing, what they like, what they don't like. Third, do a little research—see if they need help, move obvious obstacles, and make space for them at the table. Fourth, incorporate people with disabilities into the group: my church invited me to apply for a small group leader position and chose not to move forward in a way that honored me. Finally, advocate for those with disabilities and share their burdens.

While many of the same principles are helpful for children's ministry, there are some differences. Adult ministry is generally more flexible than the highly structured ministry contexts that serve children. A few guidelines will ensure kids with disabilities feel welcome in your children's ministry.

Use the buddy system to pair an adult volunteer with a child who may need extra assistance during children's programming. We strongly urge against separate classes for children with disabilities. This teaches younger children that those with disabilities are "other" and socially non-normative. In fact, having separate classrooms for people with disabilities could potentially create the feeling of isolation. Also, the asset could feel the people serving in that ministry are only doing it to check a box. We want to work toward a *whole church* mindset, one which trickles down from the leadership throughout the entire congregation. In other words, as we discuss in the next section, PWDs should be a part of the church community from the pulpit to the pew.

"Twentieth Camper": Jake and Julia's Stories

I spent my summers working at a camp—tossing dodgeballs, opening the Scriptures, and laughing about everything with my second- and third-grade campers. We would set up camp at a different church each week, run our programming, and head out to the next one. As such, local volunteers were critical; we wanted campers to get connected with adults in the local fellowships.

In our last week of camp, the camp director pulled me aside and let me know I would be getting two volunteers, which felt like a refreshing jump into the pool after a long, hard summer. When my director told me that one of them, Julia, had cerebral palsy—which impacted her both physically and mentally—that refreshing jump turned into an icy bath.

My workload as a summer camp staffer had suddenly doubled in size. Immediately, I began to stress. I wasn't qualified. How would my campers react? After I met Julia, some of my fears subsided. While her struggles were legitimate, her level of independence was high, even if I struggled to understand her sometimes. Yet, even after meeting her, she remained the "twentieth camper" in my mind.

On Wednesday, we shared the gospel with the campers. After my explanation, Julia jumped in and asked if she could share her story. I hesitated. We only had a few minutes left of Bible study. After a short pause, I relented. In her own way, she shared how she became a Christian. When she finished, I hurried to usher the campers to the next activity. As we lined up, I saw one of my campers step out of line and walk up to Julia.

This camper and I had a few discussions earlier in the week about making mean comments about Julia, so I prepared myself to fix the problem.

But Julia smiled. And laughed. And then she looked at me and gave me a little thumbs-up. The camper stared at the carpet as we walked to the next activity. Julia grabbed my hand and asked if she could talk to the camper during the transition time.

"Of course. What did he say?"

Julia smiled again. "He wants to become a Christian. He just doesn't know how."

My jaw dropped. Embarrassment flooded me. In my mind, Julia's ministry had been an inconvenience—yet her story had reached someone I never could. By the end of the day, the camper had made the decision to follow Christ, and my perception of ministry changed forever.

———

Find ways to make games accessible. Certain curricula such as Grow Kids include accessible games. If possible, it is best for everyone to participate in the game in the exact same way without modification for the asset. If the game is modified, it is possible the modifications themselves might highlight the asset's differences. In some cases, kids are disgruntled by the special treatment the asset can receive. Consider playing games all the children can enjoy without modification, such as trivia or board games.

Your most valuable resource will be parents and guardians. They know their children better than anyone else. Listen to their advice and create a plan for success. Many ministries have individual plans for the child's spiritual growth. On your student intake form, gather information about the child's bathroom needs, communication level, and assistive devices. However, also ask about what activities the child enjoys and where they are in their relationship with God.[3]

---

3.   Beth Golik, "14 Questions to Ask on a Student Intake Form (Plus One I Never Ask)," Key Ministry, June 7, 2023, https://www.keyministry.org/church4everychild/2023/6/8/podcast-episode-054.

PEWS AND PULPITS

Previous chapters have discussed how churches might make it easier for PWDs to fill their pews, but churches must also consider how PWDs might fill their pulpits and why PWDs should be represented in leadership positions. What if we saw people the way God sees people? A church or ministry needs to hire staff. They search for what type of person? Someone who is strong, gifted, and successful by the world's standards? Does a person who has it all together rise to the top of the list? Or does the interview committee press into each resume and interview each candidate to determine the best fit for the congregation's needs? Many ministries look for people with a track record of winning, those who easily attract others or present themselves as dependable, resolute leaders. Rarely do we inquire about someone who is weak and dependent. But we should. David Deuel, Senior Research Fellow for the Christian Institute on Disability, believes God works powerfully through our weaknesses and infirmities. He writes,

> By God's design, he chose Moses, Isaiah, and Paul in weakness and disability, then sent them on their missions. Was this mission sabotage? By no means. God used their weakness to disable pride, dismantle opposition and display his power to a watching world. If the church's mission needs weakness, the church needs to allow people with disabilities to express their call and giftedness for the glory of Christ. They will demonstrate the value of weakness, as well as the need for weakness. Shouldn't we pray for a greater presence of disability and weakness in the church?[4]

If those with disabilities are truly to become normative members of the church, they must be represented in every area—from the pews to the pulpits. How can churches help fill the vacuum of pastors representing the community of those with disabilities? Some may have an instinctive

---

4.   David C. Deuel and Nathan G. John, eds., *Disability in Mission: The Church's Hidden Treasure* (Peabody, MA: Hendrickson Publishers, 2019), 17.

response: hire more PWDs. They think, "When visitors see a pastor with a disability, will they not feel welcome? Will that not solve this problem?" Two issues arise from that response.

The first issue, hiring PWDs because they have a disability, disregards their actual skills and gifts. That disregard toward their skills and gifts labels and promotes PWDs based on a single attribute: their impairment.

Secondly, hiring people with disabilities does not necessarily change the social and physical environment. Consider yourself a budding angler. Your pond has a surprising lack of catfish, but you are hoping to have a population within the next year. So you go out, purchase some catfish, and toss them into the pond. Have you not solved the problem? Soon, however, you find your catfish floating belly-up. What went wrong?

Your pond is a saltwater pond. Catfish live in freshwater. You have tried to solve a problem without knowing the true problem. Hiring someone with a disability just to hire someone with a disability may introduce them into an environment that is not prepared for them. Problems might lurk beneath the surface that have not been addressed, and those problems could pose real sources of harm toward the newly hired PWD. Instead of hiring someone with a disability *because* of their disability, churches should first fix their culture and their facilities. When the culture is normalized and those within the congregation are intentional about making friends with assets, only then will the church be whole from the pews to the pulpits. Hiring someone with a disability may put visitors at ease. However, be wary of fixing one problem while leaving the main problem unaddressed.

Another problem which needs addressing is the lack of students with disabilities seeing full-time vocational Christian ministry as a viable option in their plans. Where do pastoral staff come from? Most still come up through the ranks of Christian colleges and universities, seminaries, and Christian grad schools. We need a concerted effort to recruit and train students with disabilities. We need to assure they are welcomed and warmly invited to study at our training centers. In so doing, future generations of students with disabilities will see more people with disabilities who have undergone biblical training serving in active ministry capacities.

One of the schools that stood out in our research was Western Theological Seminary in Holland, Michigan. Western is one of a very few seminaries to offer a graduate certificate in Disability and Ministry. Julie Myers, the first graduate from that unique program, possesses a passion for serving assets along with their families. She notes a critical factor concerning assets' families—the disability impacts the entire family unit, and so our care for the asset needs to address the entire family unit.

Another powerful tool Western Seminary uses to educate future pastors and Christian workers on the needs of the disabled community is their Friendship House.

> In 2007, the Ralph and Cheryl Schregardus Friendship House at Western Theological Seminary became the first seminary housing of its kind. Friendship House is a pod-style apartment complex where 18 students live alongside six young adults with cognitive disabilities, and the partnership has led to astounding results.

> Friendship House gives the six Friends an opportunity to live independently and work in the community, while the seminarians get the opportunity to learn what it means to live alongside someone with a disability. We at Western Theological Seminary would be diminished without the presence of our Friendship House Friends. They have enriched the lives of seminarians and given us a deeper appreciation of all people and a deeper understanding of what it means to be human.[5]

Julie writes, "I love living in the Friendship House with my kids!" she says. "Although it has been difficult, God has blessed us abundantly over and over again."[6] In 2018, the six "founding" Friends graduated. They transitioned to new living arrangements, making room for new Friends to come live at the house. "The Friendship House has inspired other seminaries to create

---

5. "Welcome to the Friendship House," Western Seminary, accessed June 22, 2023, https://www.westernsem.edu/welcome-friendship-house/.
6. "Testimonial from the First GCDM Graduate," Western Seminary, accessed June 22, 2023, www.westernsem.edu/academics/degrees/graduate-certificate-disability-ministry /#toggle-id-4.

similar communities. Duke Divinity School started their own Friendship House in 2013, which was followed by others at Vanderbilt and George Fox University, another in Fayetteville, NC and soon, one at the University of Aberdeen in Scotland."[7] At Liberty University's School of Divinity, undergraduate students are now able to get a degree in Bible or religion with a focus in disability ministry. The program was established to help students develop a theological foundation for understanding disability ministry and the practical implications for specific ministry contexts.

Imagine how powerful it would be for a future pastor to live for a year or two with someone with a disability. Do you think they would be more sensitive and understanding of the needs of the disabled in their community and especially in their own flock? Absolutely! May more Friendship Houses spring up at Bible and Christian colleges and universities across the nation and around the world. May seminaries and Christian graduate schools launch more programs and degrees which include disability studies in their regular curriculum.

A Researcher's Insight: Dr. Erik Carter

Erik Carter has devoted his life's study to research and writing on faith and people with disabilities. His landmark study on belonging noted that

> disability must become a deeper part of the dialogue within seminary and continuing education. More than 21 million families in the United States have at least one relative with a disability and most people will personally experience a disability at some point in their lives. Yet future clergy and ministry leaders receive limited preparation related to serving and supporting this segment of their community well. In their study of North American theological schools, Annandale and Carter reported that the topic of disability made limited appearance in the seminary curriculum, opportunities for direct involvement in the lives of people with disabilities and their families were infrequent, and the extent to which students

---

7. "Welcome to the Friendship House."

with disabilities were well supported on campus varied. Most concerning was that three quarters of seminary leaders felt that their graduates received little or no preparation to either include people with disabilities into multiple dimensions of congregational life or to address the spiritual questions related to disability. Congregational leaders are influential factors in the degree to which the dimensions of belonging . . . will be pursued and supported. Strengthening their commitment and confidence in this area is an important investment.[8]

DISABILITY AUDIT

When parents bring home their first baby, they are asked to conduct an infant audit of their home. Literally, they are asked to get on their hands and knees and crawl through the house. Why? To see their home in a fresh way. To view it through the eyes of an infant or toddler. Are there electrical plug-ins needing to be capped? Are there bottles of chemical cleaning agents that could be mistaken for something to drink? Could a wobbly bookshelf fall over if pushed? Things taken for granted by a thirty-year-old might prove disastrous to a small child. In the same way that new parents go before their infant, we urge you to walk through your school, church building, or organizational meeting space with fresh eyes. One of the classes in our alma mater required non-disabled students to take on and "live with" a disability for a few days. Some students chose hearing loss and plugged their ears. Others wore blindfolds to simulate vision loss. Others tied an arm behind their back or chose a wheelchair. Two responses typically followed: acknowledgment of difficulty and deep embarrassment.

When pressed about their embarrassment, many students relayed how it felt wrong to "pretend." However, after a few days, many students realized something even more profound. Yes, they felt embarrassed. But they were embarrassed because everyone thought they needed help when they really

---

8. Erik W. Carter, "A Place of Belonging: Research at the Intersection of Faith and Disability," *Review & Expositor*, 113, no. 2 (2016): 167–80.

did not. They were embarrassed because their needs did not match their perceived level of independence. Not only was it physically demanding, but it was socially, mentally, and emotionally exhausting as well.

For this disability audit, we suggest you do the same. While it may be tempting to engage in an audit during the week, we challenge you to do so during a worship service. Only then can you empathize with both physical and social stress. Our audit has four phases.

Phase One: Approval and Communication

In phase one, before you conduct the audit, be sure to contact and gain the "go-ahead" from everyone in your church leadership. Clarify that the point of these exercises is to enact change. If you have anyone with a disability in the congregation, get their permission as well. Those with disabilities are experts (assets) in navigating your facility; take their advice and listen to their concerns. Some churches may gain enough insight from these assets that they do not need to progress to phase two (although we will recommend it, as it is the only way to have an informative phase three). Finally, be sure to inform the congregation that an audit will be taking place.

Phase Two: Audit

In phase two, conduct the audit. Begin the process before you leave for the worship service. If someone needs to drive you because of limited mobility or sight, arrange for it. Do not stop the audit for inconveniences; if you stand and stretch every time your body gets sore from sitting in a wheelchair, you have failed to understand the normative experience. These are only a few ideas. If assets in your congregation have other ideas, prioritize them. When the auditor has returned home after the church worship service they may remove their gear. Use one of the scenarios below:

1. Hearing loss: Wear earplugs or earbuds with noise-canceling functionality.
2. Vision loss: Wear a blindfold, dark sunglasses, or remove corrective lenses.
3. Limited mobility (lower extremity): Use a wheelchair, crutches, or a scooter.

4. Limited mobility (upper extremity): Tie an arm behind your back. (Allow a coin to decide which arm; those who have lost a limb rarely get to choose.)

5. Sensory processing disorder (hypersensitivity): Wear earbuds that relay outside noise but turn up the volume all the way; you can also do this with hearing aids.

Phase Three: Reflection

Reflection takes three forms in this phase. First, reflect personally, directly after the audit. Do so privately and honestly. Do you have a headache? How does your body feel? Who in the world kept poking you before service? A week later, after another worship service, do a second private reflection. What changes did you see after experiencing a "regular" service again? Did you appreciate simple things once taken for granted, like the doors, more? What were you more aware of? Did you ever figure out who was poking you?

Third, reflect publicly. Ideally, one to three weeks after the audit, share your findings with members of your community in a forum. Prioritize inviting assets already within your community to the forum as the experts. Prepare to answer questions, concerns, and ideas from your congregation. Many churches are unprepared to welcome someone with a disability, and an audit can be met with hostility. Some may even be hurt by it. Others may believe you are "making fun" of PWDs. Some may be confused why someone disrupted the service with such a "ridiculous spectacle."

This kind of audit not only illuminates changes that should be made in the physical facility, but also those needed in the church culture, as well as in the auditor's mindset. An audit provides an opportunity to draw attention to the issue. Hostility often illuminates underlying assumptions or pain that can be addressed by pastoral staff. An audit also gives assets the ability to serve their community as leaders and experts in the field.

Phase Four: Action

Implement change. Every church will be different. Consider the feedback from your assets, from your forum, and your private reflections. Plan. Many, when considering a disability audit, assume the auditor will be sitting in the audience. This can be immensely helpful, as statistically most visitors and congregants with disabilities will be sitting in the audience. However, if a vision of full inclusion means welcoming people with disabilities from pew to pulpit, why should she or he have to sit in the pews? Work with assets in your local assembly and leadership to see if having your lead pastor conduct the audit might be a beneficial challenge for your congregation.

To conclude this section, the auditing process serves as a key step helping shift the daily rhythms of the church or parish closer toward the rhythms the Bible envisions for the regular life of the church. The audit allows local congregations to detect the physical and social barriers hindering people with disabilities from serving the local church—from the pews to the pulpit. The audit also aids the recalibration of the local congregation's mindset toward full inclusion for people with disabilities. Additionally, it allows leadership to detect blind spots in their own thinking as well as the thinking belonging to the people they shepherd, so the leadership can address those areas.

Overall, the audit sharpens our eyes to see people with disabilities and the challenges they face in a new light, which is exactly what our next chapter focuses on: what it means to truly and honestly *notice*.

Part 3

THE FIVE-STEP PLAN
FOR BUILDING
GENUINE FRIENDSHIP

So far, we have explored how the disability community has been viewed historically, potential physical and social barriers within churches, how the Old and New Testaments view disability, and how churches might conduct a disability audit. Before we move on to how our churches might become communities of belonging, a point needs to be addressed. All people experience the feelings of loneliness, depression, and a lack of value. But, these feelings can be intensified for assets because belonging requires actions that can be difficult, if not impossible, for them to pursue. That's why with our Five-Step Plan, as you will see, we focus on the handler building a personal relationship and eventually friendship with the asset. This process can be long and hard, but ultimately reaps tremendous rewards.

Chapter 7

NOTICE

The disability community is vast, and the struggles are myriad: work,
transportation, health care, housing, faith formation, and education to
name just a few of the challenges common throughout the community. While organizational and political advocacy for PWDs has a critical
place in the Christian response, many individuals may not have the resources to initiate change in those arenas. We do not pretend to solve
all the intricate disability issues and accessibility problems. Some may
live in a very small town or an isolated, rural area with very few social
support programs, churches, or organizations to assist those with disabilities. Everyone, however, can be an individual advocate, working to
create a little sphere of *shalom* within their communities.

Our application is aimed at individual advocacy which, in turn, spurs
cultural shifts. We want readers to expand the mission of the church by
working at building an authentic, growing friendship with a person with
a disability. We call this our Five-Step Plan.

The Five-Step Plan works to bring real help and healing to those in
the disability community who are vulnerable to isolation and misunder-
standing. In addition, the plan helps promote Christlikeness because Jesus

spent so much of his ministry reaching out to the broken and suffering. As pastor Dane Ortlund asks, "How do we care for a wounded body part? We nurse it, bandage it, protect it, give it time to heal. For that body part isn't just a close friend; it is part of us. So with Christ and believers. We are part of him."[1] That is the posture the church is called to bear toward all who are hurting, including our brothers and sisters with disabilities.

NOTICE

Are you a people watcher? Do you enjoy sitting at the airport simply *observing?* What type of person do you readily notice? Our eyes naturally move toward the beautiful, the successful, the wealthy, the gifted or talented, and the powerful people among us. We post images on social media of our interactions with athletes, movie and television stars, and business or political leaders. We follow those same people and funnel their glamorous pictures into our feeds and timelines. If a photo gets posted and makes us appear weak or awkward, we might consider pressing the delete button. We prefer doctored images of ourselves. Filters help hide our flaws.

When we walk into a banquet hall, what type of table do we seek? We might inquire if we can sit toward the front, or at the table with the speaker, or near the important people. Not the table situated at the back of the room, populated by a sparse group of people dressed in drab colors. This book, and this chapter, turns those ideas and tendencies on their head. As a part of linking up with God's strategy for highlighting what God's strength can accomplish through our weakness, we are asking you to continue focusing on the *least* among us. Jesus himself advocated eschewing the rich and famous when planning a banquet. "But when you give a feast, invite the poor, the crippled, the lame, the blind" (Luke 14:13). Our banquet-planning strategies ought to mirror the way Jesus planned parties.

As has often been stated, the journey of a thousand miles begins with the first step. In this chapter, we explore the first step in our Five-Step Plan, some common objections and hesitations to step one, and, finally, some practical tips to make step one a little easier and more effective.

---

1. Dane Ortlund, *Gentle and Lowly: The Heart of Christ for Sinners and Sufferers* (Wheaton, IL: Crossway, 2020), 41.

Step 1? Notice. Noticing is not simply *seeing* a PWD, the asset. It is seeing that person with intentionality, observing not only the fact that they are present but also what potential assistance that person might need and, physically, how well they are able to interact with others. This might be akin to creating and executing a play in football. You can think of this section of the book as a handbook or a playbook, a systematic approach to building and maintaining an authentic friendship with someone with a disability.

We cannot work toward building disability-integrated churches, schools, and organizations if we do not first notice people all around us who have disabilities. Whether we realize it or not, people with disabilities possess incredible, God-given gifts, passions, and talents, many of which have yet to be unleashed. Too often we are blinded by disability. Pity wells up as our first reactive emotion, or we patronize or engage in a fear-based response. Rarely do we slow down long enough to really notice. "Tell me about your dreams. What do you do best? What did you want to be when you were a kid? What are you longing to become?"

While the concept behind Step 1, Notice, is one of the simpler action steps to understand, its importance cannot be overlooked. Once in college, when I (Jason) attended a Hanukkah party, I became separated from the main group because physically I could not get close enough to them with my power chair to continue the conversations. At this party, they were serving a light meal and I needed help getting food. I was ignored for a large portion of the evening until Kevin saw me and noticed my needs. Kevin's noticing my needs led him to inquire, and he eventually assembled my dinner. If you had attended this party, you might have *seen* me, but would you have *noticed* me? Would you have perceived my predicament?

Another incident during this same evening sticks out in my memory. I had a conversation with someone from the college group at the church where I was attending. I mentioned I was feeling extremely isolated. She said, "Why? I see you all the time!" Since we were discussing the importance of noticing, I asked, "But do you ever interact with me or engage with me?" Her silence answered my question.

These stories highlight two common issues those of us with disabilities often face: first, the problem of forced or unplanned physical separation from a group; and second, the issue of others merely seeing a PWD but never intentionally noticing them. Seeing alone does not always lead to noticing in the manner in which we are employing the term *noticing* here. Seeing alone is not enough. In the story above, Kevin demonstrated he not only saw the person but also acted upon his observation.

When I (Jason) attend parties like these, I am consistently isolated and alone. Rarely does someone notice my predicament. Other PWDs I have spoken with relay similar stories. Those of us in the disability community have a tendency toward isolating ourselves from social events. When we receive invitations to social activities, we sometimes think, "Ugh, is it worth the hassle? Will anyone see and notice I am even present? Or will I once again be ignored?"

This loving act of noticing, however, begins to undo some of the psychological baggage of the persistent thought, "Why am I even here if no one sees me?" I know Jesus is the friend of the wounded heart, but I sometimes wish more people adopted Jesus's view. I wish more of God's people were friends of those with wounded hearts, that more of God's people noticed the people in their lives who carry wounded hearts.

We are often told in Scripture how Jesus saw and noticed. It is a comforting thought to know *God sees* (Gen. 16:13; Ps. 11:4). I am glad Jesus knows what I am going through. But sometimes I want *another* person to see and notice my plight. Jesus will build his church. He is building his church, and he is using you and me. He is asking us to notice people. Imagine building a house without a door or a window or skipping the roof. This is what happens in the church body when we overlook or ignore people with disabilities. The church is not all that she can be when we shut out and isolate large parts of the disability community, shutting out and isolating large parts of the body of Christ.

Again, seeing is not the same as noticing, which is the first step in our Five-Step Plan. Try this exercise the next time you attend a social gathering. We are certain some of you already do it: scan the room from time to time, looking for someone who is present at the event who looks isolated or alone. Is there a way you can strike up a conversation? If they appear to be struggling, can you engage them with an offer to assist? It is worth the awkwardness to simply inquire, "Would you like me to help you get more iced tea?" or "Can I introduce you to my friend?" It may be uncomfortable at first. Someone may misunderstand your care or concern. Your kind overture may be met with a stare or awkward silence. Press on. It is one of the reasons we flirted with the idea of calling our book *Getting Past Uncomfortable*. This title was suggested to us by Dr. Erik Carter, the disability researcher quoted earlier who serves at Baylor University. One day, after you have built a God-ordained, deep friendship, you can look back and laugh at any awkward, initial exchanges. "Remember the first time we met, and I spilled iced tea all over your power wheelchair?"

Before we articulate a few common objections and hesitations to this first step, we want to dispel some popular myths. The first myth? Assets are often alone and isolated because they want to be. This is not always true. Sometimes a physical location itself necessitates our inability to be present with a group. Think of a baseball game at a stadium, a concert at an arena, or a beach near the ocean. If I am blind, deaf, or struggle with Down syndrome, these places are not easy to navigate. If a person struggling with any one of those disabilities chose to remain on the outskirts of the scene, it would make sense. But maybe with a friend serving as travel companion, they would or could venture out. How much better it is to enjoy the trip with a trusted friend! You never know till you take the first step and notice.

At other times we are unable to physically engage with the selected activities. We might not be able to run a 5K race, play paintball, or zip through a dark haunted house. And sometimes, perhaps cruelly, we are told that we are in the way! Once I (Jason) was talking with a friend while attending a college group gathering. Meanwhile, during our conversation, the door greeter kept telling me I was *in the way*. Even though there were several large groups in the same relative area, she said nothing to them. Perhaps selfishly, I overreacted and wheeled to the opposite side of the room so I would not be accused of *being in the way*.

These are a few of the reasons people with a disability sometimes feel alone and isolated. We do not often purposely choose to be alone and isolated. Occasionally, the physical location just does not work. And of course, no one enjoys hearing accusations of being an impediment to the good time others might otherwise enjoy. To repeat, simply seeing a person with a disability is not enough. We must work at noticing. Are you willing to get past the uncomfortable and reach out to a potential new friend? Ask God to help you take the crucial first step.

To offer a different perspective, when I (Paul) attend a party, because of my ADHD, I feel the need to run around the room, quickly hearing from each person present. Also, when I interact, I often cut others off or finish their sentences. And, unlike Jason, I wouldn't *dream* of sitting home alone and missing a party! When the music is playing, food is being served, and there are *so many people* present with whom to interact, well, it's heaven for those of us who crave chaos. *What in the world . . . there must be twelve different appetizers here . . . I believe I'll try one of each!*

However, like Jason, I also need a friend present to assist. I often need an honest companion to inform me, "Hey, Paul, that guy was trying to tell you a story, but you kept interrupting." Or a good friend who can let me know, "Paul, are these your coat, phone, and car keys that I've found in several different rooms around this house?" It helps when someone *notices* I'm struggling.

One of the problems with simply seeing without actively noticing someone is that seeing without noticing creates what we might call *a trophy syndrome.* When this happens, the person with the disability, the asset, is admired or fawned over for their presence alone. This syndrome rears its ugly head in churches or organizations where a group wants a PWD to be present at events so they can claim, "*See? We are inclusive. Do you not see our friend here who has a disability?*"

Trophy syndrome grows progressively worse if the asset is asked to speak or share with a group, with the goal of the church or organization members being motivated or encouraged. Unfortunately, they often do not engage people with a disability on the terms of a deep, authentic, friendship-level relationship. This creates the uncomfortable situation where, over time, the PWD begins to feel they are like a painting, brought out to show off but not to be interacted with at heartfelt levels. The asset begins to feel like nothing more than an object.

Perhaps they are seen as a beautiful trophy—a trophy of grace, but a trophy nonetheless. This ends up turning into what Stella Young, a comedian and journalist, calls "inspiration porn." Those with disabilities are often objectified by those without disabilities as ideals of perseverance and hard work. However, as Young points out, this exploits those with disabilities for the benefit of those without disabilities.[2] People with disabilities are often used as pawns for inspiration.

Another reason why simply observing or seeing is not enough is because with simple observation, there is no way to communicate to the PWD that you *know* they are present and that you *care*. In a way, this hesitancy to notice could possibly be born out of a fear that those noticing a person will be judged negatively if those noticing are accused of staring at a person. This leads to an overreaction when no offense is meant. The person being observed might wonder, "Why is this person staring at me and smiling? Why don't they just come over and chat with me?" More than likely, they hope that the person standing over there, teetering on the edge of noticing, chooses to approach them.

What are some common objections and hesitations to noticing people with disabilities? In the next two sections, we'll explore common concerns. Jason will answer the objections, and I (Paul) will explore the hesitations.

POTENTIAL OBJECTIONS

Objection #1: "What if the asset wants to be left alone?"

Jason: Well then, the potential handler should approach the asset and ask! Do not pretend to be a mind reader. Take the first step and walk across the room. "Pardon me, you may want to be left alone, and if so, no problem; however, I wondered if I could ask you a couple of questions about your power wheelchair?" Personally, I would much rather entertain an awkward question than sit alone in silence. I prefer embarrassing conversations over uncomfortable stares.

---

2. Stella Young, "I'm Not Your Inspiration, Thank You Very Much," TEDxSydney, accessed June 23, 2022, www.ted.com/talks/stella_young_i_m_not_your_inspiration_thank_you_very_much.

Objection #2: "How does the handler avoid jumping to conclusions and stereotyping?"

Jason: We dive into this topic at length in our Step 2, Engage, but suffice it to say, in general you should talk to the asset like you would anyone else. For example, jumping to a conclusion might sound like: "Hey, Jason, I saw you sitting over here by yourself so I could not help assuming you must hate these parties as much as I do?" The answer is that I really enjoy socializing. So I sometimes employ humor and reply, "No, actually, I love parties! It's just the rest of the group went downstairs, but you probably noticed there is no elevator in this home . . . my dumb luck!" My humor gets a little crazy by necessity.

Objection #3: "What if there's no one in my group of friends to notice?"

Jason: First, there may be more people with a disability around you than you might think. It is a common phenomenon; once someone is exposed to something in a new way, they begin to see that it exists everywhere. It is like when someone buys a green car. They then begin to see green cars everywhere. This is a major purpose of our book: to give you this initial exposure so you will see people with disabilities all around you and not only see them but *notice* them. Even in the small chance there is no one near you with a disability, you can still implement our plan with people who are isolated, lonely, or discouraged. Look around your school, neighborhood, or church; we are confident you'll begin to see and, hopefully, *notice* people with disabilities everywhere.

OVERCOMING HESITATIONS

I (Paul) will have to admit I sometimes ignore or fail to engage persons with a disability for selfish reasons. I am afraid I might needlessly offend. I will consider sheepishly offering, "Hey, can I push you across the room?" And, in my imagination, the person in the power wheelchair responds, "I can get across the room by myself!" From my work with Jason and my research for this book, I have realized the risk is worth the potential momentary embarrassment.

Other times I am fearful I may make a mistake when trying to be friendly or help. For example, if I offer to assist someone who is transferring into or out of a van or car, I worry, "Do I hold them around the waist? Do I let them stand on their own? Was that the correct way to help?" These hesitations are often easily resolved, as I learn to simply ask, "Hey, what's the best way to help you move from your chair into the van?" Or, even more basic is the question, "Would you like me to help you get into your van?" You might think these are ridiculous. But we are guessing you have some of your own fears.

Another potential hesitation is the fear my first offer of help will be taken as an offer to become a volunteer, long-term caregiver. I sometimes think, "If I give them a ride this morning, they will need a ride every morning." Or "If I pick them up for worship service this Sunday, I will be committed to giving them a ride *every* Sunday." Again, I've now learned the best way to help is to be simple, honest, and vulnerable. "I am not sure how often I will be able to do this, but could you use a lift to campus this week?"

Another best practice which helps allay this fear of feeling that, by simply offering to help, you are signing up for a lifetime contract is to become part of a team effort. In our small group at our church, we enjoyed hosting a visitor, Nan, who used a wheelchair and was unable to drive. This woman became a valued member of our Sunday morning church class. However, most of us were unaware that only one family stopped each Sunday morning to provide Nan a ride. You might guess what happened over time.

The lone helping family grew weary of the task. What started as a lovely offer of assistance turned into a burden. We should have set up a team approach where several families rotated the carpool. Not only could this have freed up the lone family, but several other families could have enjoyed the blessing of getting to know and help Nan, and she could have enjoyed the blessing of getting to know, at a deeper level, several members of our class.

Many of you provide ongoing, long-term care to a person with a disability. God bless you for your faithful service. Some of you assist from time to time when you are able. You know both the joys and frustrations volunteering often provides. Others of you want to jump in and help but are not sure where to begin, or fear offering to help may overtake your life. Examine your own hesitancy and fear. You see a person with a disability, but do you hesitate to really notice? Why or why not, and how might some of our stories help you overcome your hesitations?

SOME PRACTICAL TIPS

A helpful element when considering Step 1, Notice, is to train yourself to have a wider field of vision. When we are speaking with someone, it is always best to give them our undivided attention. But try not to fixate solely on the person you are currently speaking with. We all gravitate toward socializing with our closest friends, with whom we are comfortable. We urge you to also observe others and practice looking around for someone who may need your attention. As you scan a room or a particular setting, shoot up a prayer and ask, "Lord, is there anyone here you want me to notice in a new way?" "Is there anyone here you want me to see through your eyes?" Broadening our perceptual awareness has many positive effects and is crucial for connecting with potential assets and outsiders.

If you find yourself hesitant or in fear of engaging with a person with a disability, there is no shame in taking your time and observing. However, the plunge must be made. God wants to use you. He desires to spread his loving care and concern in and through you. He will use your feet to take the first step and walk across a room. He will use your tongue to speak healing (Prov. 12:18). God wants to use your arms to help a blind person across a room and your hands to push a wheelchair into a sanctuary.

If you are in any type of leadership position with a church, parish, school, parachurch, or nonprofit organization, we urge you to consider ways you can engage your members and constituents in volunteer service for those with a disability. The options are endless. Find out what organizations are effective and sign up for training or offer to serve. Ask the leaders of the disability ministries if they offer to help train the handlers. See people in your community who need noticing. Jesus said, "When you give a dinner or a banquet, do not invite your friends or your brothers or your relatives or rich neighbors, lest they also invite you in return and you will be repaid. But when you give a feast, invite the poor, the crippled, the lame, the blind, and you will be blessed, because they cannot repay you. For you will be repaid at the resurrection of the just" (Luke 14:12–14).

We have seen how employing Notice as the first step of our Five-Step Plan relies on more than just *seeing* the asset. To really notice someone requires intentionality and planning. We have also explored some potential objections and road bumps to noticing as well as some possible solutions. Step 1, Notice, is a necessary first step to complete for the handler to assist a potential asset. Notice can often instantly dovetail with Step 2, Engage. But an outcome of Notice is that the groundwork for a successful engagement is laid. Notice is the step that can be completed in the shortest amount of time. Simply put, observe an asset, where they are and what they are doing, and then proceed with an honest inquiry. God will bless your servant-hearted effort.

Chapter 8

ENGAGE

To reiterate our vision, we see churches, schools, and organizations waking up to the sleeping giant that is the untapped potential and giftedness belonging to PWDs. We are calling upon ministry leaders to more often notice and engage persons with a disability and to turn away from the practice of pushing people into a corner or siloing them into specific categories. The goal is for the full integration of PWDs into the beloved community, allowing PWDs to use their gifts and talents in new and refreshing ways for the benefit of the body and the glory of God. Employ everyone to carry out the mission, regardless of status or position. This is what David Deuel calls "weakness pressed into service."[1]

In the last chapter we discovered the first step of our plan, Notice. But the strategic action plan does not culminate there; the potential friend or handler will naturally move forward with Step 2, Engage. In Step 1 we noted that seeing is not the same thing as noticing. Here, we are saying noticing is different from engaging.

---

1. David C. Deuel and Nathan G. John, eds., *Disability in Mission: The Church's Hidden Treasure* (Peabody, MA: Hendrickson Publishers, 2019), 24.

The key element of engagement revolves around asking good questions. To start, ask if you (the handler) can introduce yourself and meet with the person with a disability (the asset). In our experience, this is radically different from the conventional mindset. The conventional mindset seems to be that the assets normally ask to engage and integrate themselves with their friends or peer group. The onus in the conventional model rests with the individual with a disability. "Is there anyone who might be able to help me attend the concert next Friday night at the super-arena?" Flipping that status quo provides freshness and relief to the potential asset. Rather than the burden resting on the asset who might feel shame or guilt when it comes to asking for assistance, the potential handler makes the first move, and it is a social move that helps alleviate some of the pressure felt by assets in social situations.

There are several problems with the current approach of some well-intentioned disability ministry efforts. Many times, there are limited places and spaces in which an asset can physically participate. For example, in the lunchroom of my undergraduate school, I (Jason) was only able to sit at one side of one of our assigned tables because my power wheelchair could not fit in between the two tables. So, as much as I wanted to join the group on the other side, I physically could not. Similar occurrences happened when the group was in the basement at a party I went to at a professor's house. I really desired to join my peers, but I was not able to.

Once, some quick-thinking members of a seminary Greek class were able to manually ferry my wheelchair up to the professor's movie theater room. I felt like I was sitting atop the ark of the covenant. I was able to really fit in and enjoy the evening with the others.

At another similar event, as a member in a men's choir, the loft where we sang was not accessible. In fact, the only way to access it was to climb up about four flights of stairs. Four guys in the men's choir regularly carried me in my manual wheelchair up to the choir loft and then transferred me to one of the seats. Because of their actions, I was able to fully participate.

However, in these positive instances, my presence at these events was not because of my actions but because of someone else's initiative. Someone cared enough to approach me, help me, and offer to give of themselves. In their actions, whether they realized it or not, they were acting like Christ, who did this for each of us. On my own, there was no way I could have maneuvered up the choir loft steps in my power wheelchair.

After the potential friend or handler introduces him- or herself and begins meeting the person with a disability, other questions should be asked which are quite normal—even obvious! "What's your background? What do you like to do? What's your favorite movie?" These are all quite frequent questions, but ones that are often overlooked or skipped due to the presence of a disability. One of the questions that is extremely important at this stage, and forms a foundation for the others, is asking questions about an asset's impairment. The friend could ask questions such as "What do you need help with?" or "I have noticed you using a walker. What disability do you have? How does it affect you?" When I posed these questions to my friends during my initial research, they expressed a lot of uncertainty about them—namely, would asking the questions cause offense or hurt feelings? These concerns are understandable, but in my experience, not realistic. Allow me to explain.

I have been living with cerebral palsy for as long as I have been alive. (Well, minus a few hours because my disability occurred shortly after birth. But I do not typically count that because I cannot remember that far back.) For me and others like me who have lived with disabilities all our lives, our disability is inseparable from us. We are more than our disability, but it cannot be separated from us in any way. Our entire lives, and even our outlook on life, has been impacted by our disability.

I would love to be able to walk up the stairs and not have to worry about whether the elevator is broken or watch a choir practice walk-through and not have to wonder if there is an accessible entrance. But that is not my reality. Because of this, I and others like me enjoy it when others inquire about our disability because it shows they possess a genuine interest. Plus, I know they have questions about my disability. Over time I have answered every question imaginable about my cerebral palsy.

When someone like you asks about my disability, I feel you genuinely care. Often when I talk about the various difficulties of my day, people who overhear me think I am just complaining when, actually, I'm just stating what happened. The potential friend asking about my disability gives me permission to share my burden with them in some small way. This is what we are called to do. As Christians we need to bear each other's burdens. God is in our story—even in the broken parts. He knows our specific needs. He wants to use the "able-bodied" to assist the "disable-bodied." And he wants to use the "disable-bodied" to help meet needs of the "able-bodied." We need the Lord, and we need each other, able-bodied and disable-bodied.

People asking honest questions lays the groundwork for the development of organic friendships. Their good questions demonstrate genuine care. This is one of the reasons why I love it when small children approach me. What do you think their first question is? Many times, they begin, "How did you get to be in the chair?" Children possess the uncanny ability to ask what everyone else is thinking because they have not yet developed a proper social filter. This is one of the reasons why Jesus so loved their company. Young children are not often bound by social anxiety and paralyzed by fear like so many adults. Kids often blurt out the obvious. Their unbridled honesty is refreshing.

Asking what an asset likes to do, in conjunction with their physical limitations, allows the handler to create a framework for upcoming activities. Without the knowledge of what the person enjoys, finding realistic activities, the point of the third step, Research, is impossible. Discovering actionable activities, without a knowledge of the person's physical limitations, also proves incredibly difficult. Step 1 can occur quickly. But Step 2 takes time. Consistently meeting the person, talking to them, listening, showing them that someone cares, that they are loved and wanted, takes time. It is difficult to openly engage with someone when we have ingrained the learned behavior of staying quiet or getting out of the way. This is the biggest concern about moving to Step 2. For much of our lives, people like me, PWDs, have been told they are in the way, blocking everyone, and that they should remain quiet. Also, PWDs may not verbally communicate it but may consistently demonstrate the idea that help is not needed.

Plenty of times in my life I have been given a task on a service team just to keep me busy. For years I went as the devotional leader on my church's service trip to West Virginia. I enjoyed participating and I am indebted to the service leader for making a way for me to go on those trips. That is where my love for teaching flourished. Despite all these positives, however, when the thirty-minute devotional time was finished, there were still twelve hours of volunteer work left—work I couldn't fully participate in. They gave me the job of painting a post that still had to be redone after I had finished. On this same mission trip, we were assisting with a fundraising sale. I was told to go in the corner so I would be out of the way. When I asked for something constructive to do, the answer I was given was that I should pray. (This caused me to have a shallow view of prayer, which was not rectified until I read a popular book on the subject by E. M. Bounds.)

On the other side, I have experienced churches unwilling to give me any sort of opportunity. At one church that I attended regularly as an undergrad, I had met with the college pastor and asked him if there were any potential service opportunities. I specifically suggested any sort of teaching or speaking roles that might be needed, knowing that occasionally they had guest speakers address the small groups. He said that he could not think of any opportunities for me specifically. The next week, one of my peers who had been involved in the worship team was given the opportunity to teach. This is a perfect example of what I like to term the "pay your dues" process in churches, where in order to be noticed for positions, one has to work their way up and do random service tasks. While this may work well for the average person in the church, it is near impossible for an asset because we cannot physically do a lot of the entry-level service activities, So most of the time, we are practically unable to serve because we can't get noticed and prove ourselves. Some time later, the same pastor had given a brief lesson on being involved in serving the church. I immediately went up to him and said, "I would love to be more involved," hoping to rekindle the conversation. He immediately responded without missing a beat, "I think you are involved enough." In the past two years of my active involvement in that church, I had only been given *one* opportunity to serve and that was to visit a shut-in at a rehab hospital who wasn't even there when I went. When he said this, my first thought was, "Would he say the same thing to one of my fellow peers? I highly doubt it." Surely there were more ways for me to serve the church!

Step 2 concretely demonstrates care when someone outside the PWD's immediate family chooses to be present. A key point about this step? The handler is not forced to hang out with the asset. Disability research shows family members can become bitter over feeling they must continually provide care. Further, in many disability programs the person with a disability is assigned an able-bodied buddy with whom to hang out. This approach is better than no friendship, but it sometimes leads to the feeling that the person is only doing it because they are volunteering for an agency or the organization. The forced friendship can once again feel like seeking a box to be checked.

Now, we might assume they would not be volunteering unless they cared, but this type of forced companionship is often all a person with a disability sees or feels, and it makes us feel we are simply an inanimate object to be served. Or sometimes the program feels constructed simply to make the person serving feel good about themselves.

In this regard, Step 2 becomes more than simply asking questions. Asking routine, simple questions is a wonderful starting point. But handlers must move toward developing a dialogue. They must open up and share about themselves, too, so assets continue finding points of common interest. In this way, the handler becomes a devoted friend. Ideally, like other authentic friendships, interpersonal communication is not limited to one situation or location.

How deep can we go if we meet only once a week at the same time and location?

We encourage a natural and organic approach. As this occurs and develops over time, the asset realizes they are much more than a number or a project to be worked on, because they are shown legitimate care. The asset realizes this care goes beyond words, and the time the handler spends with the asset builds trust. That genuine trust will be necessary for the following steps in our plan, allowing the asset to drop their guard and let the grace of God enter the friendship.

As part of Step 2, I (Jason) need to mention that most PWDs have plenty of experience asking for help. We must ask daily to accomplish even the simplest of activities like eating or getting dressed. The only way I was even able to work on this book was through my scribe, Amanda

Jarus. But it is much more refreshing when another person notices we might need help and then asks.

Notice I said "ask" and not "do." The asking puts the ball in our court. There are some times when I want to struggle through an activity because I am still able to do it. If a person were to immediately jump in and perform that task, it would rob me of the opportunity. Asking communicates that the handler notices we are struggling and gives us the freedom to determine whether we need their help. This process of giving and receiving helps brings a little more humanity back into our lives.

Even though I normally do not have a problem asking for help, sometimes it is still hard—just like it is for you. Especially when I am in a crowded area and do not know anyone's name. I and others like me sometimes have problems reaching out to others, not just because of physical barriers but also because of some social ones. I spent my early life as an only child mostly isolated from my peer group. Therefore, it is sometimes hard for me to break into group conversations and ask for assistance. The helpful friend, not only noticing I need help but going on to ask, helps remove this stressful element of the encounter.

If the handler has spent years with an asset, the question no longer needs to be asked. But in the beginning stages asking is a necessity. When in doubt, it is always better to ask. Asking if we need help will not offend us—in fact, just the opposite. If the handler or others around us remain silent, it causes us to wonder if we really are seen. Sometimes I play a little game to test the people around me. I do not ask for any assistance, and I wait to see if anyone will notice that I need help, for example, pulling a chair out of the way so I can pull in or helping me with a plate of food at a church potluck. I am pleased to say that, especially recently, those around me have passed this test with excellence.

Unfortunately, this was not the case while I was growing up. This test is a double-edged sword. It reveals if there are any who notice my plight. It shows if the emotions directed toward me result in actions and are emotions that are more than words alone. As seen in the Hanukkah party example above in Step 1, throughout my life, many people would say they loved me and wanted to be there for me. But these were the same friends who in high school wanted me to be in a corner and stay quiet;

they wanted nothing to do with me. I was too judgmental, since we were all adolescents, but that is how I felt.

The real purpose of the Five-Step Plan, as you will notice, is to break through a lot of the social trauma and emotional baggage the asset has built up over the years. The goal is for the asset to fully experience their status as a beloved child of God, created in his image. True care begins to emerge at this stage of the plan, Engage. Francis Assissi paraphrased Rule of 1221, Chapter XII, teaching that even when one is restricted from preaching, they can demonstrate the love of God through their actions. This is founded in James 2 where believers are exhorted to demonstrate their faith through action, especially in loving others (James 2:14–18).[2]

If you need any more encouragement to begin this step, think about who Jesus spent time with. Were they not the tax collectors, sinners, outcasts, the blind, and the lame? Jesus did not always seek to associate with the influential and the wealthy, but with those whom society had cast out. Jesus did this to demonstrate his love and care for them. I am not advocating that we never make connections with those who are rich and powerful. In fact, this is how many helpful ministries and organizations are started and sustained. But at the same time, we should pay special attention to those who, in society's eyes, would never be able to repay our service or our giving. We serve, not because of requirement and necessity, but because of genuine love and care. This is the very heart of God.

As you reflect on our challenge, ask God to show you someone toward whom you can practically demonstrate this love and care. If he has not already, ask that God would create in you a desire to care and show love to the person with disabilities, to show Christ's grace and concern fully and completely.

One of the purposes of the Five-Step Plan is to bring awareness to those who have no idea about the scope of the opportunities in the field of disability ministry. We hope this process will cause the handler to move from mere acquaintance to genuine friendship. This often occurs at the point of demonstrating care. Our hope is that many more will catch the

---

2.   Rule of 1221, accessed February 15, 2024, https://www.franciscanthirdorderpenitents.com/rule-and-constitutions.

vision of offering love and care to a person with a disability in the concrete form of building an authentic friendship. To those of you who already serve in this field—may your tribe increase!

In the next chapter, we will cover Step 3, Research. Unless you engage with a PWD, listening to their dreams and needs, you will not be able to conduct the research needed to display further care toward that person. Furthermore, you will lack the friendship that sustains this mutual relationship.

Chapter 9

RESEARCH

At this point in our book, you may be asking, "Okay. I agree. We need to fully integrate people with disabilities into all aspects of the life of the church. And I agree I need to build an authentic friendship with the asset. But what is the *asset* supposed to do?" In our highly motivated, overly measured, success-oriented church culture, we often wonder what task or assignment people with a disability will be able to *perform*. Because, really, our utilitarian society asks: What use is someone if they cannot *accomplish something*?

Dr. Benjamin Conner, director of the Graduate Certificate in Disability and Ministry at Western Theological Seminary in Holland, Michigan writes of appreciating the "ways that people with intellectual and developmental disabilities participate in bearing witness of the Spirit in modes that aren't necessarily rational or linear, programmatic, or dependent on the capacity for abstraction or verbal communication."[1] There is a freedom for people with intellectual and developmental disabilities to participate

---

1. Benjamin T. Conner, *Disabling Mission, Enabling Witness: Exploring Missiology through the Lens of Disability Studies* (Downers Grove, IL: IVP Academic, 2018), 104.

in showing who the Spirit is, sharing portrayals of the Spirit that people without intellectual and developmental disabilities struggle to envision. Conner explains:

> The church follows the dominant culture in *homogenizing* people with ID [Intellectual Disabilities]. As should be clear by now, disability is a complex and heterogeneous concept, and ID is no different. It can be mild to profound; some people with intellectual disabilities can hold a job, and others can't hold a cup of tea. Some have the capacity to interact with others as self-determining agents, and others are responsive in ways that are barely discernible to those who don't spend hours with them. Within the church, people with ID should be empowered to participate in the life of the congregation to the extent that they desire, and their capacities and gifts allow them, just like everyone else.[2]

In chapter 7 we encouraged you to Notice. In chapter 8 we asked you to Engage. Here, we undertake a bit of Research. When we use the term "Research," we primarily refer to the handler doing the advance work of determining if a specific location or event will be accessible to the asset as well as to others in the group. (This is like the disability audit mentioned earlier.) Secondarily, we will discuss the size and scope of disabilities in the general population. Statistics vary and are understandably difficult to measure. However, we can capture a look at how many of us in the United States have disabilities by sifting through the data.

The type of research we ask you to undertake on your adventurous journey toward building new friendships requires the handler to scout places where friendships and group interactions may best flourish. There are two types of research in this vein: passive research and active research.

Passive research is when handlers, having gained a preliminary understanding of the asset's likes and dislikes as well as their limitations, notice as they are going about their daily lives places where the person with the

---

2. Conner, *Disabling Mission, Enabling Witness*, 105, emphasis added.

disability could and would want to attend. These could be concert halls, sporting arenas, or church sanctuaries. This is a constant, low-level effort of research that speaks more to the handler's mindset than anything else. On the other side of the coin is active research.

Active research is when the handler—knowing the potential activity the friends or friend group wishes to attend, for example, a concert or a museum—proactively tests the routes and accessibility. They check to make sure there are elevators throughout the stadium, ramps on the sidewalk, or subtitles at the movie theater.

For example, say you meet up on a regular basis with someone who struggles with blindness. You best serve them and build the most authentic friendship by learning more about their struggles. You may engage in reading a book by a blind author. You may conduct informal interviews with blind people or those who assist them. The help lists are endless but include:

- going through a day with your eyes completely covered.
- learning to read braille or listening to audio books.
- discussing with your friend how you might best assist in crowded spaces.
- researching additional health challenges which accompany blindness.
- helping with walk-throughs of new spaces that will often be used.

Many do not understand the extent of this need for research. A church I (Jason) attended had just established a disability ministry. I reached out to the disability coordinator and said I would appreciate someone researching the places where the activities were to be held. The disability coordinator replied, saying, "You need to do the research on your own." Maybe he did not know or was unaware that I could not access many of the places that others were suggesting.

On another occasion, we were having an off-site church picnic that I really wanted to attend. I did not know, however, if I would be able to physically get there because Chicago has some paths that are completely inaccessible. Thankfully, I ran into two people who helped me navigate the location. Once I got there, the same disability director said, "I am so glad you made it." My snarky, automatic reaction was, "You didn't do anything to help." Because of the director's responses, I perceived that despite him saying he wanted me to be there, his actions told a different story. The main problem with pinning the research step on the people with disabilities is that it is difficult for them by themselves to determine if the location is accessible. Really accessible. Not just marked accessible online. You are probably getting the idea. In Step 3, the handler can be a huge help in simply *going before* the asset or group to smooth the way by checking for obstacles or hindrances which might ruin an otherwise wonderful event.

Once, a family member called a doctor's office asking if it was accessible. They were answered *yes*, but we arrived only to find a large front step. When we asked how I could get in, they said, "We usually just lift up the chair." But my chair—a power wheelchair weighing more than 300 pounds—cannot normally be lifted over a large step.

Remember our earlier note on both passive and active research. *Passive research* is gaining an understanding of the likes and dislikes as well as the physical capabilities of the asset. The handler, going about daily life, notices the locations that would be both accessible *and* match both people's interests, the interests of both the asset and the handler. This level of research should constantly be occurring and requires only a slight change of mindset.

Active research occurs when the handler hears about an activity and proactively checks to see whether the route is acceptable. They take the path the asset would take, ensuring everything is accessible. Simply calling ahead is helpful but often not sufficient.

Active research requires more work and intentionality, but the more work that is put into this step (and all the steps, for that matter) illustrates practically that the person with the disability does indeed matter. Active research makes tangible the truth that the asset is precious, beloved, created in God's image, and a valued member of the body of Christ. As the handler pursues more and more active research, time after time, the trust level and comfort that the PWD experiences goes up. The asset can relax. They do not have to be constantly on guard when it comes to outings or social events. Because they trust the handler's track record, they do not have to wonder if they can truly participate in an experience.

One of the major difficulties belonging to the Research step is that the handler must be intentional in their research. Active research can involve a considerable time commitment, but this time commitment is necessary. If you do not have time right now to engage in Step 3, let us encourage you, at the bare minimum, to Notice and Engage.

Because of the time commitment, you should limit implementing the Five-Step Plan to only two or three people with a disability. We encourage you to start with one person and not be afraid of failure, because even if you try this step and fail miserably, you are still a better friend to the person with a disability. They will remember you and your friendship for a lifetime.

There is something you need to know about me. I (Jason) have a horrible sense of direction. If it were possible, I could get lost on the way to the rapture. On my first time leaving Chicago to go back home to Florida, I had to go through O'Hare International Airport. My mother and I had traveled from O'Hare to my Bible college, so I knew it was possible. But I could not remember which train stop we took. A dear friend tried to find the route to O'Hare via the train map. We had a map of all the transit stops, which outlined which routes and stops were accessible. He found a stop near us marked *accessible*.

But when we arrived at the stop, we encounted a problem. No, the elevator wasn't broken—it did not exist! When my friend went down to talk with the train station attendants, they assured him that the elevator had never existed at that location. It was mismarked in the literature. This experience solidified for me the necessity of someone physically going to a route and location ahead of time. It is not enough to depend on maps and phone conversations.

During my time at college, I regularly cut through our music building to get to the cafeteria. I enjoyed multiple opportunities to bond with the music department desk workers and music students. I mentioned my love for orchestral music to one of the guys in the chorale. He mentioned an upcoming concert at a local park. I told him my fear of being unable to attend due to accessibility issues. He promised he would travel the route beforehand to ensure that it was accessible. I agreed to go because I enjoy attending classical concerts and was relieved that someone would help me get there.

When the time for the concert arrived, it became clear he had traveled the route intentionally. He told our traveling group we needed to use one bus station over another because one had an elevator. This was the first time anyone outside my immediate family showed they cared about me, and not just in words but in actions too. My friend's actions made me feel valued and like a full participant of the group. We desire for all people to experience these feelings, especially those who have a disability! We can all be kind to others. Part of taking an extra step of kindness is showing others the love of God in Jesus's name.

Another important point to remember is the humility sometimes required by an asset to admit they need assistance. As mentioned above, disabilities such as autism or ADHD can carry shame. Who enjoys arriving at an airport and announcing to a gate agent, "Pardon me but I (Paul) have ADHD and all these flight cancelations and delays are quite disorienting"? I feel the person in line behind me is thinking, "Oh for goodness' sake, out of *all* the people at this airport, I got stuck behind the dummy who can't read the arrivals and departures board!"

When I (Paul) was studying Greek and Hebrew in seminary, I *loved* the tutoring sessions offered outside regular class time. It doesn't take long to learn you don't want to be the person in class always raising their hand and requesting, "Hey, Prof, can you cover the steps to parsing an adjective once again, you know, for those of us with ADHD?" Most tutors I've met are patient and kind, possessing the gift of slowing down and listening well. These godsends often ask kind questions such as, "Okay, does everyone have it or should we go over this again? It's really no trouble, and we have time left."

This is one of the reasons schools provide accommodation for those with disabilities. Whenever I (Paul) experienced an academic examination with a one-hour time limit, I was always astonished when students turned in their exams in the first few minutes. Meanwhile, I spent the first few minutes looking around the room wondering why a particular student was absent, what book the professor had chosen to read during our exam, and why the facilities team never greased the air conditioning fan that squeaked when the room was otherwise silent.

Because of God's amazing grace, schools today have moved forward in their thinking and planning. Thankfully, we now hear opening comments provided at academic examinations that begin, "While we've budgeted one hour for this exam, we understand some of you may require extra time, so take as long as you need." Whew! Music to our ears!

A potential objection arises here. Is it not possible for the person with a disability, the asset, to conduct all this research on their own? In fact, I (Jason) was explaining this step to one of my peers and using it to illustrate the difficulty of finding and visiting churches. I was expressing to him how difficult it is for me because I never know if the paths, roads, and sidewalks to the churches will be accessible. And, even if they happen to be, will the churches themselves be accessible? I offered a scenario: "In the dead of winter, in downtown Chicago, with the brutally cold wind whipping off of Lake Michigan and snow falling, can you imagine if I am forced to turn around and go home?" His response? "Well, you just have to take that risk."

The main reason a person with a disability often cannot research potential outing locations on their own is due to a legitimate fear. "What happens if I get trapped somewhere?" It is impossible for me, for example, to go up the stairs of a building and ask if there is a back way that is potentially accessible. Sometimes I do not see potholes or mud divots until my wheelchair falls into them. I need someone's help to make me aware of them. The final reason PWDs often fail to conduct the research is the psychological barrier we have established. Often, we feel alone and isolated—like no one cares—so why seek out new places to go if no one wants to go with us anyway? I will admit, I fall into the trap of thinking, "They never want to come with me so why should I research anyway?"

The next objection I commonly hear often pertains to churches, but also to various activities with groups of friends, namely that the person with the disability is never involved, so why should the friend put forth the effort to conduct the research? This can be a vicious cycle. A person with a disability rarely attends because there is not much for them to do. Or in relation to churches or ministries, the activity is often not accessible, or it is not communicated that it is accessible.

The last objection is that all this investigating and researching is too hard and too much work. On the one hand, I agree with this; it *is* a lot of work, extra time, and a sacrifice. But this mindset betrays the thought that the person with a disability *is not worth the effort,* and, as such, this is a transactional mindset toward the handler-asset relationship.

I am glad that mindset is not the one Jesus held. He saved us despite our sin. While we were God's enemies, he paid the ultimate, humiliating sacrifice by dying on a cross for our sins. He had every right to remain in heaven with the Father. Yet he emptied himself and lived his life as a servant. His sacrificial act expected no reciprocity. In a very real sense, then, the handler practically shows the attitude of Christ to the person with a disability, the asset. But the asset cannot pay it back, in most cases. When Jesus discussed who to invite to a wedding feast, he mentioned paying special attention to the poor, the blind, and the lame, inviting them to feast as opposed to those capable of repaying the favor.

The easiest way to practically apply this step is to *do* it. As you are going about your everyday life, observe the places around you through the eyes of someone with a disability. Note the many barriers to people with disabilities, such as stairs, narrow hallways, or a lack of elevators. The more time the handler spends with the asset, the more intuitive these advance scouting missions become. You build up your reconnaissance muscles. And the more the friendship develops, the greater the understanding the asset will have about how much the handler really cares.

If this is your first time considering disability and the surrounding issues, it can all become overwhelming. Let us encourage you not to let that stop you from putting the Five-Step Plan into practice. At this point, we have covered three of the five steps of the Five-Step Plan. Before proceeding, take stock of where you are now. If you are at Step 1, great! Now work forward toward Step 2. If you are already building friendships or asking questions, wonderful! Consider moving on to Step 3, Research.

If you are one of the rare people looking at locations for accessibility, God bless you! You are ready for Step 4, Incorporate. But no matter where you are in the Five-Step Plan, it is best to do *something, anything,* rather than nothing because, for many PWDs, a new friend taking a genuine interest in their plight reflects the love of Christ. Someone working at developing friendship and building trust is a gift from God. Get past uncomfortable and take that first step by making a *forever* impact on someone's life.

Chapter 10

INCORPORATE

"Hey, wait a minute," someone asks. "Is it possible this Five-Step Plan could help to build an authentic friendship in other challenging contexts? Ministry among people experiencing homelessness, someone struggling with sexual addiction, or a person who has been caught in a cycle of incarceration?" The answer is yes. Use the Five-Step Plan in whatever contexts God moves you to use it. In this book, we advocate employing the plan with someone who has a disability. Why? Because we see, along with many others, that this is a historic moment when our culture is focusing on the disability community. Churches and ministries are asking how they can better minister to people with disabilities and their families. Seminaries, Christian colleges, Bible colleges, and Christian graduate schools are for the first time offering degrees and programs in disability studies. Also, we have found that there is very limited discussion on building relationships with people with disabilities, especially those with physical disabilities.

Thankfully, we are moving past the days when we viewed anyone with a disability as someone who needed fixing. PWDs should be celebrated, not shamed. PWDs should be listened to, not ignored. Those with disabilities give us relief in knowing we do not have to strive for the exhausting, elusive goal of perfection. There are no perfect people, churches, or ministries. God rejoices when we humble ourselves and discover, explore, and even embrace our weaknesses. We do not have to grovel in shame when we make mistakes. Imperfection is a part of life. Knowing you will occasionally mess up frees you up to own up to your inherent frailties and to lean into God's arms.

It is always best to remind ourselves: He is the Creator. I have been created. He is the Potter. I am still on the wheel. He is God. I am human. He is mistake free. I am mistake prone. He exists perfectly. I get along imperfectly. Consider how often the Scriptures remind us to embrace imperfection as a lifestyle:

- He gives power to the faint, and to him who has no might he increases strength. Even youths shall faint and be weary, and young men shall fall exhausted; but they who wait for the Lord shall renew their strength; they shall mount up with wings like eagles; they shall run and not be weary; they shall walk and not faint. (Isa. 40:29–31)
- But God chose what is foolish in the world to shame the wise; God chose what is weak in the world to shame the strong; God chose what is low and despised in the world, even things that are not, to bring to nothing things that are, so that no human being might boast in the presence of God. (1 Cor. 1:27–29)
- For I decided to know nothing among you except Jesus Christ and him crucified. And I was with you in weakness and in fear and much trembling, and my speech and my message were not in plausible words of wisdom, but in demonstration of the Spirit and of power, so that your faith might not rest in the wisdom of men but in the power of God. (1 Cor. 2:2–5)
- For the sake of Christ, then, I am content with weaknesses, insults, hardships, persecutions, and calamities. For when I am weak, then I am strong. (2 Cor. 12:10)

Some disabilities are temporary and can be helped or even healed. Someone may recover from a stroke or serious illness. Other disabilities are permanent and degenerative—completely life-altering, such as an amputation or a horrific accident. And still others can sometimes be better understood as differences, as author and poet Daniel Bowman notes,

> Neurodiversity's gifts do not form a discrete list. I think they are ways of being, of approaching our days; they are lenses through which the autistic person sees and feels the world uniquely— lenses that can lead to helpful contributions to culture. In my case, my autistic brain wiring leads me to see storytelling and poetry and teaching and learning and worshiping God in ways that are different from what most readers will be accustomed to.[1]

OUR GOAL AND STRATEGY

Let us review our goal. We urge full participation from persons with a disability in every area of church life and ministry as those persons are able and feel so led. We promote friendship building between persons with a disability (assets) and the able-bodied (handlers). What we are fighting against are barriers, both physical and social, which reduce this much needed participation. Any local church, ministry organization, or Christian academic setting which fails to welcome these beautiful gifts of disability and diversity suffers from being *less than* the ideal. Our strategy for reaching this lofty goal is the creation and implementation of our Five-Step Plan, which can be used either within or apart from each of these settings. These budding friendships possess a powerful carryover effect. They cannot help but permeate other relationships in a growing, outward-facing circle.

For quick review: In Step 1, Notice, the handler notices the asset as well as their everyday surroundings. In Step 2, Engage, the handler engages with the asset, introducing themselves and asking honest questions. In Step 3, Research, the handler researches potential locations and activities for the asset and their community to engage in experiences together. Step 4, Incorporate, brings all the previous steps together.

In Step 4, the handler goes to the larger group, whether an academic setting, workplace, small group, or local place of worship, and presents the

---

1.   Daniel Bowman Jr., *On the Spectrum: Autism, Faith, and the Gifts of Neurodiversity* (Grand Rapids: Brazos Press, 2021), 38.

opportunities for communal participation they have discovered. Ideally, these are spaces and activities in which all can fully participate.

At this point, hopefully, the group agrees to take part in the various activities. Then the handler can approach the asset and mention an activity they can do with everyone else. Not only is the invitation welcomed, but the entire group has considered and bought into the idea. Finally, the handler asks the asset if they would like to take part. Asking allows the asset to take ownership and helps remind them of their human agency. This is a win-win situation for all involved.

This is an ideal example of how our Five-Step Plan can work in one typical scenario. Consider the alternative. A group of friends decides upon an activity which may or may not prove accessible to all. Everyone in the group is excited about the upcoming event. As the day and time of the event approaches, someone raises the question of accessibility. At the last minute, the uncomfortable truth is confirmed: people in the group with physical disabilities will not be able to attend. There are two possible results: Everyone except for those people with disabilities attends anyway, leaving the assets behind and engendering hurt feelings. Or the entire event is canceled and blame toward those with disabilities begins to trickle into the group's conversations as the reason why. Even if those blame-placing conversations never come into play, those thoughts and feelings that the event would have been possible if it had not been for those who were not able to go may still exist.

Before I (Jason) get into any further detail, I want to make some observations clear. This approach to Step 4, Incorporate, turns the standard activity-planning sequence on its head. Normally, well-meaning people approach PWDs and ask a blanket question, "What can you do as far as an activity?" While this question has good intentions, the problem with asking it of the asset at the Incorporate stage is twofold. One, oftentimes assets do not know the existing options in which the group might be interested. A subproblem here is the activities the group normally enjoys might be ones the assets might not be able to do. The assets might think that if they posit an idea outside the norm, the group would just be doing it to check a Christian box, not because they want to engage in a different kind of activity.

The second difficulty is that assets spend much of their time in isolation. The events, games, and activities they regularly engage in are often solo. As such they do not necessarily possess a repertoire of group activities from which to choose. The handler in Step 4 becomes a liaison between the main group and the asset. An important function of the handler is to make sure the asset is connected and not isolated during the activity.

A negative example regarding this fourth step occurred during my sophomore year at college. I (Jason) had to spend eight weeks in the hospital because of complications from a broken medical pump. I was feeling especially isolated because no one on my dorm room floor visited me in the hospital during those eight weeks. When I mentioned to the resident assistant that I was feeling lonely, isolated, and disconnected, his first response was, "I have fifty guys on the floor—I can't be concerned about one." His initial response reinforced the feelings I already had, feelings of being devalued. This sentiment was confirmed when I talked to one of my friends. I asked him directly if the other students on the floor viewed me as a burden and limitation to their fun. Sadly, he answered, "Yes." Both responses made me feel it would be better for everyone if I just moved away from the floor. I wonder how many others, like me in that moment, feel that way?

A few weeks later, however, our annual "sleep*brover*" occurred. This was a time right before final exams where everyone on the floor stayed up to 3:00 or 4:00 a.m. playing video games and loud, raucous music. Unfortunately, I could not join in any of these activities. The video games they preferred were all too fast-paced for someone like me with cerebral palsy.

In the middle of the four-plus-hour stint of "sleepbrover," the resident assistant announced, "Hey everyone, we are going to play a strategy card game." We were only two minutes into the game when one of the guys asked, "When can this game end so we can get back to what we want to do?" This statement shocked me because (1) they were not willing to spend even thirty minutes on an activity we could all undertake, and (2) they did not want to do the inclusive activity but were being forced. This reinforced the fact I was not wanted.

I often had the feeling I would be the limiting factor if I proposed something, that my suggestion would not be anything the group would want to do and would not allow the best possible outcome. It is this feeling that causes me, and others with disabilities, to withdraw from group activities. Can you see how stepping in as a friend at these important junctures would make a stark difference in the life of a person with a disability? *You* can be that friend!

This is specifically why the role of the handler is so important at this step. It is to specifically challenge the psychological barrier which often emerges in the mind of the asset, whether based on reality or not. This is the insidious idea that whispers, "They do not really *want* you to be there; they are just proposing this event out of pity." So it is especially critical to present the activity in the most helpful way: "Hey, we have already discussed this event with everyone in the group and 100 percent are on board . . . so, do you want to jump in and join us?"

As far as activities are concerned, the ideal is one where everyone attends the event, plays the game, or enjoys the activity in an equivalent manner. When a game is adapted or altered, the asset can end up feeling isolated, or their peers could accuse them of cheating. Secondly, in competitive situations, there is no way to tell who won, since everyone is playing the game differently. It can defeat the sense of camaraderie, especially if the asset has a competitive drive.

Another story emphasizes the importance of the five steps working as a whole and reinforces the truth Jesus emphasized in the Gospels. "One who is faithful in a very little is also faithful in much" (Luke 16:10). I often felt isolated in my church's college-age group. I felt I was being ignored. Sometimes I was asked to "get out of the way." Noticing me is a small action. Engaging with me is a small step in building a relationship. Spending time with me would have been a small way for someone to demonstrate care. These little things build toward authentic trust rather than expressing platitudes that make themselves look good.

In conversations with the pastor, I expressed my desire to engage and serve. At that time, I had only served once in two years. He mentioned that he thought I was active and serving quite regularly. Once, he had noted I had the aptitude for teaching. I mentioned my desire to teach and lead one of the Sunday school classes, which was taught by students. He said he could not think of any upcoming teaching times or opportunities. The next Sunday, a person who at the time was my personal care attendant and who was also involved in the leadership team spoke on the topic of integrity. This was ironic because he happened to have the bad habit of clocking in even when he knew he was unable to assist me. He was getting paid for work which was never done.

This unfortunate story illustrates how, as previously mentioned, some churches tend to hold a "pay your dues" mentality. Let me explain what I have observed. To be involved in what is considered bigger and more important service, like teaching or leading, one must demonstrate commitment by doing perceived "entry-level" service—greeting, setting up chairs, or cleaning up after an event. For a person with a physical disability, a lot of these opportunities are almost impossible. This prevents such people from climbing the ministry ladder and being noticed.

This was the experience I had in the group where this next story comes into play. Every summer the church held a college retreat, and the college pastor wanted me to come along. I really wanted to attend. But because my church's college group was not faithful in the small things before, I did not have the assurance that they would be faithful in this larger commitment. I changed my mind because of all the extra effort and orchestration I would have to deal with: personal care attendants, transportation issues, and medical reasons. They did not demonstrate themselves faithful enough to show care through talking with me, why would they now make a greater commitment? The pastor wanted me to come, but to what end? What would be my benefit? It certainly was not for fellowship.

Also, I reasoned, if the group regularly ignored me on Sundays, what would cause them to notice me on the retreat? A lot of the activities on the retreat were physical, like paintball, a ropes course, and hiking. When I talked to my peers, they agreed most of the activities were physical, but some people stayed in the cabins because they did not like them.

There is a difference between not participating in activities because you choose not to rather than because you are not able. It makes assets feel like we are missing an essential comradery. This story illustrates the necessity of always keeping Step 4 in mind. Leaders, please, always remember this piece of advice prayerfully offered from a person with a disability: some activities in which *everyone* can participate should always be scheduled.

This pattern of including everyone helps demonstrate to the asset that the group genuinely wants them. If the all-inclusive events or activities are only offered once a year, then they can quickly become a check-the-Christian-box idea. Also, as Step 4 is being offered consistently, it builds confidence in the asset where they can build trust and begin to take bigger risks themselves. In this story, if the group had been engaging in this step consistently, I would have looked forward to going on the summer retreat because I would not be isolated and alone. It is more painful for an asset to go where everyone is having fun and they are alone than simply to be alone, which is why we tend to isolate ourselves, hiding ourselves from the pain.

"More Than Ramps": Alex's Story

I graduated from Dallas Theological Seminary in 2007 with a degree in biblical counseling. I moved back to Michigan in 2008 to live with my family because living independently was a great challenge for me. I would like to thank my West Michigan church and community for helping me embrace my personal and pastoral identity over the last 16 years. It is and has been an ongoing process. As a person with cerebral palsy, I have both abilities and disabilities. Both are learning tools, and they come together as a package deal. I am no longer sorry that I cannot present one without the other. I am learning to accept and integrate both my strengths and my weaknesses day by day. Being me is both a daily struggle and a daily delight.

I walk with forearm crutches, and I use a wheelchair when I must travel long distances or keep up with people whose normal speed is not slow. I need my friends and family to help me drive, cook, clean, and comb my hair. There are parts of my life which are not typical, but there are other parts of my life which are. To know me is not only to see what I can't do, but also to see what I can do. Every day, I engage myself in listening, learning, praying, and loving. I have wonderful parents, spectacular siblings, four charmingly handsome nephews, and friends who are serving Jesus all around the globe. I love coffee, tacos, coloring, reading, and my elderly Bichon dogs.

To include and accept people with disabilities is to get to know them. The reality is we all have difficulties as broken people living in a broken world. Some difficulties and disabilities are just more prominent and visible than others. By God's grace, I am growing in my knowledge of him and seeing that he can use both my brokenness and my beauty to bless me and bless others. Life would be boring and mundane if every day and every year were just the same and nothing ever changed, grew, or was dreamt about.

I have come a long way in my journey with disability, but I realize there is more work yet to be done in and through me. As a disability advocate, I long for people to recognize that accessibility is not just about ramps, elevators, and hearing loops. Accessibility is about attitudes and intentionality. Advocacy engages both agency and empathy—using my voice and my gifts to help you use yours. Am I willing to lean into you so I can learn from you? Are you willing to lean into me so you can learn from me? Can we have coffee, tea, or a Coke together soon so that we can share smiles, stories, successes, and stresses? This is real life. If I show up as the real me, will you meet me there? His mercies are new every morning and his compassion never fails. We are God's masterpiece created anew in Christ Jesus to do good works. We can keep moving forward in the awesome mission we share together to the glory of his name.

———

As Step 4 is being conducted, a genuine friendship is solidified. A positive byproduct of this step is finding a group and community where the asset and handler can mesh. In fact, in some cases, this can be a function of the handler. This will help events and activities naturally become more organic.

A POTENTIAL OBJECTION TO INCORPORATION

In my (Paul's) way of thinking, not all activities can be undertaken by every single person in a group. Say a group of campers decides to go swimming. If someone in the group cannot swim, or does not want to swim, that one person should not prohibit the rest of the group from enjoying swimming. A group of friends may wish to attend a concert at a large arena. As far as possible, every effort should be made to accommodate someone with a disability. However, if no accommodation is available I (Paul) believe the group should still attend.

What I understand my coauthor and friend, Jason, to be arguing for is the insistence that people with a disability stop being overlooked. Many of us have treated people with disabilities as second-class citizens and have failed to incorporate them into every area of life. This is sin. Hopefully, this is changing as more churches, nonprofits, parachurch organizations, and schools recognize the need to include persons with a disability in every area of their vision and mission. In addition, as we learn about the gifts of neurodiversity, we learn that good and godly people think and reason in differing ways. Diverse ways of thinking are to be celebrated.

My wife and I raised five children. With seven in our family, we were busy. I remember, at times, turning down some exciting opportunities for want of each child being able to participate in them. Any parent who has enrolled their child in sports programs will recognize this scenario. Imagine one of your children plays soccer, and they end up being talented. They score a few goals and help lead the team to a string of wins. What comes next? One of the parents inevitably learns about a more important soccer team and asks if you want to be involved. This team will consist of elite soccer players from the area. This team will have better coaches, will play against tougher competition, will travel to other cities for tournaments on the weekends. You get the picture. What are you to do? Even your child is asking to join.

For our own family, we determined that all five of our children should be able to experience extracurricular activities. Therefore, we decided not to let one child take on the extra responsibility of joining up with a super-team, which might exclude one of their brothers or sisters from participating in their own. Our reasoning: if one child were to emerge as a super-athlete, there would be plenty of time for that gift to grow and develop without having to force the rest of the family to disrupt their lives.

I like Step 4 because the handler can approach the group with various ideas and activities that could include everyone. This does not preclude a group from occasionally enjoying events on their own, even if the person with a disability is unable to participate. However, it is the mindset of thinking of others as more important than yourself we are promoting here (Phil. 2:3–4). Again we mistakenly think, "Well, it is Disability Sunday—what could we do this year that everyone could enjoy?" This is the same mindset that reasons, "Hey, we have a few persons with a disability attending our church. What if we offered a Tuesday evening class where they could all meet up with each other?" Segregation often works against incorporation.

The better goal should be starting with the asset first and discovering their God-given gifts, interests, and passions. Then together you can incorporate those good gifts into every area of church or parish life. Persons with a disability are not burdens to be partitioned off into a corner. As Christians we should not promote members gathering in a disability district. They are gifted image-bearers who bring insight and wisdom to all. They should be fully integrated into every area of the life of a school, church, or ministry. We are richer for interacting with and poorer for ignoring certain people among us.

So, yes, I say incorporate whenever and wherever possible. Work at incorporating and including *first*. Design most activities where all can participate. But I can also see times when some activities or events may simply not be feasible for some. Say a group of friends informed me they are planning to summit Mount Everest. I don't think I would ask them to change their plans by selecting a slightly smaller hill I might be able to climb! I would celebrate their accomplishment and welcome them back with an activity everyone in the group might be able to enjoy. If the same group announced they were planning to climb an incredibly challenging mountain once a month, I might find a different group of friends. Or I might find ways to assist. I could oversee planning and mapping. I could coordinate all transportation and meals. I might become the team's videographer, editing the video and chronicling the climbs. The list of ways I might join in with the team, short of climbing with them, is endless.

A POSITIVE EXAMPLE

A positive example of Step 4 happened during my (Jason's) senior year at college. My scribe at the time knew I liked musicals and suggested I attend a meeting of the college music group. Without her suggestion, I would not have known the group existed. One instance from my time with that group sticks in my memory. We were watching the movie *The Prince of Egypt*, particularly the dancing scene. We all gathered in a circle just like in the movie. I stayed outside the circle and did not engage because I did not want to run over anyone's foot with my heavy power wheelchair.

However, the president noticed and encouraged me to join in, enabling me to have enough space to move without endangering anyone's feet. This positive story illustrates how being part of a group, with interests similar to those of an asset, requires someone else to provide input. In this case, that person was my former scribe. But it also required the notice and action of a key group member, the president of the group. So, here, two people helped me out. My scribe suggested the visit to the music group, and then the president of the music group suggested I join in. They both helped me incorporate into the group activity.

Another example of this type of incorporation or inclusion was illustrated in the video drama, *The Chosen*.[2] The older brother of Simon the Zealot, Jesse, is paralyzed. But Simon is perfectly able-bodied. At one point in the episode, Simon and his friends are enjoying the traditional wedding dance. But Simon notices his brother is off by himself. So he encourages his friends to move the dance toward his brother so his brother can engage and join in. This scene vividly illustrates how a person who is not disabled can serve as a bridge between the two groups.

POSITIVE EFFECTS OF INCORPORATION

Incorporating helps remove the psychological feeling of "checking the box syndrome." Whether accurate or not, those of us in the disability community often feel people might be engaging with us solely out of Christian necessity; if they could be somewhere else, they would be. Related to that, Step 4 works to demonstrate their love and concern are authentic. Often, I have been told by people that they love and care for me, but their actions do not match their words. For example, they might say, "We like that you are here. We love you. Could you go over to the corner and be quiet?" All of us hate it when this happens. From my conversations with others who are disabled, it happens an awful lot.

---

2. *The Chosen*, Season 2, Ep. 4, "The Perfect Opportunity," 02:49, accessed September 27, 2022, https://www.angel.com/watch/the-chosen/episode/82250814-1158-45b4-aae3-119aa16dcc3e/season-2/episode-4/the-perfect-opportunity.

The actual love of incorporation is demonstrated because the asset consistently sees the group cares for them and wants to spend time with them, reinforcing their importance and personhood. Step 4 also has the benefit of helping the asset feel useful and valued, especially if the activity or event is one where they can fully participate. For example, even if I cannot physically participate in all events, I can help coordinate rides, send out group announcements, or talk one-on-one with another person who may also not be able to join in.

A point of practical application is needed here. As a handler builds a trusting relationship with the asset, he or she begins to think of interests and activities that overlap. What are activities they both might really enjoy? It may also be helpful to think of communities both the asset and the handler might appreciate and mesh with. As with the other steps, it centers around honest dialogue and genuine concern.

One concluding remark needs to be made about this step. While Incorporate is the next logical step after Research, the previous steps still need to be practiced. Handler and asset are still engaging with each other, learning about likes and dislikes. Handlers are still researching to find accessible spaces. Each of these steps work together in a positive, self-reinforcing circle. Each fuels the other. The stronger the sense of research and personal connection in the other steps, the more effective this fourth step will be. As I have stated before, do not fear failure. You will stumble. Keep stumbling forward. Even the failure will demonstrate that you both, handler and asset, hold genuine concern for each other beyond simple platitudes.

A REMINDER FROM PAUL

I know Jason agrees with me on this point, but it needs to be reiterated. Our ultimate need, as handler or asset, is to fully ground our identity in Christ. Allow me to provide an illustration from the world of sports. Since I am from Kansas, I enjoy cheering on the University of Kansas and the Kansas City–area sports teams. Say the Kansas City Chiefs football team wins several games in a row. I may end up feeling good about myself. My Kansas City Chiefs have helped me feel like a winner. Then, unexpectedly and without warning, several key players on the team face severe injury. Uh-oh, what comes next?

I begin to question my very existence. I ask myself why I was forced to be born and raised near Kansas City. I wonder if the entire world is laughing at me. Once again, I pledge not to let myself fall into the trap of placing such importance on stupid sporting events that make trivial difference in the world. I finally reach an equilibrium where, win or lose, I enjoy watching my Kansas City Chiefs without feeling as if a loss is a direct strike against my identity. I enjoy observing from this position of semi-detached fan—until, perhaps, the Chiefs reel off several wins in a row, and I am drawn back in, once again, to my identity being placed in a football team.

Even our Five-Step Plan executed perfectly will always fall well short of the importance of placing your identity in Christ and enjoying his stubborn love. So, you discover your friends attended an event without you? You discover you are horrible at the game everyone else at the party is enjoying? It hurts . . . but you will survive. Someone accuses you of being self-centered or selfish? It will not be the first time . . . or the last! People can be mean. Others can bring incredible pain into our lives . . . even friends and family members. Press on. Do not isolate yourself. Allow others in. You have a reason to sing. Jesus Christ is still on the throne. God has brought you into his family.

People with disabilities will fail us. People without disabilities will fail us. Christ will never fail us. Your *asset* will fail you. Your *handler* will fail you. Jesus sticks closer than a brother. Your favorite Christian leader might fail you. Jason Epps will fail, at times, to meet your expectations. Paul Pettit will consistently fail to meet your expectations. Jesus Christ will never leave you or forsake you. In fact, Jesus is the only person who can control your life without ruining it. If you let another control your life, you will be severely disappointed. Let Jesus control your life and he will exceed expectations.

Now, due to our developing friendship, I (Paul) can hear Jason saying both Christ and other people are needed. This is not a binary choice of either placing all our identity in Jesus or our caregiver, friend, spouse, handler, asset, professor, pastor, favorite author, recording artist, or even in our flawed local church or incomplete understanding of the Scriptures. Our identity must be placed in our supreme commander, Jesus Christ, as we also reach out in faith and trust others who are willing to befriend us. We stand in Christ alone. But still, this standing with Christ does not preclude us from standing with others as well. We find our identity in Christ *as we also* go about building deep friendships and using our gifts in service.

My reluctance, and my reason for this simple warning, is to ask you to examine yourself and ask others, "Do you think I am grounding my identity in anything other than Christ?" We assume you are not, but we do not want you to develop an amazing friendship only to be incredibly disappointed when one of you stumbles and falls. Because one of you will. However, "Two are better than one, because they have a good reward for their toil. For if they fall, one will lift up his fellow. But woe to him who is alone when he falls and has not another to lift him up! Again, if two lie together, they keep warm, but how can one keep warm alone?" (Eccl. 4:9–11).

Another brief reminder. Just as there are no perfect friendships, there are no perfect churches either. Jesus Christ is the head. The church is the body. We assume since the head is perfect the body must be also. However, Jesus reminds us he is perfecting the body. He is washing the bride with the water of his word (Eph. 5:26). Jesus is currently setting apart—sanctifying—his church, his bride. Jesus is holy. The church needs to be sanctified. Why? It is filled with flawed, imperfect people. There are currently no perfect churches because they are filled with imperfect people. You have heard the old joke: if you finally stumble across the perfect church, do not join it, because you will ruin it!

Yes, the church is far from perfect. This is why we see so many Christian books arguing against racism, injustice, class envy, gender discrimination, and the host of other social ills which plague the body of Christ. God is prompting his activists and advance scouts to sound the alarm. Like Noah and his ark—he wanted his boat to be in the water, but he did not want the water to be in his boat—God wants his church to be in the world, but he does not want the world to be in his church. By using the term "world" (κόσμος) here, I am referring to the world's manner of reasoning, which is juxtaposed against God's way of wisdom (Prov. 14:12; James 3:15–17). We're working here to convince you to embrace the weak things of this world. We're challenging you to lean into brokenness and frailty. This is counterintuitive. This is the way of Christ.

The word *corpus* means "body." It is the root word of the term we are using here: incorporate. To incorporate means to join the body or bring together. It means "take in," or "include," as a part joined to the whole or "embodied." This work is a rallying cry for incorporating to a greater degree persons with a disability into the life of your local church, school, or organization.

We are also promoting our strategy of incorporating your friend, who may have a disability, into these same bodies. We make them less than they could be when we silo certain people away from the gathered body.

Yes, the process can be messy. Sure, there will be uncomfortable moments. You and I may embarrass ourselves. We will recover. The finish is worth the start. Step out in faith and push past the uncomfortable. God pushes with you.

Chapter 11

ADVOCATE

Time for a reminder. One of the main purposes of this book is providing a road map for better integration of PWDs into their local church or ministry. We are not calling upon leaders to implement a specific disability ministry program. Rather, ours is an organic approach, encouraging the creation of authentic friendships.

In chapter 7 we discussed how the handler notices the asset as well as the surroundings. In chapter 8 we focused on the handler engaging the asset with honest, open-ended questions. In chapter 9 we argued for research, both passive and active. We urged the handler to passively observe potential physical spaces of access and actively map out a plan of execution. In chapter 10, we saw the handler form the bridge between the asset and the larger group as well as facilitating connections to larger groups. Finally, we come to Step 5, Advocate, which is a natural concluding step.

In some senses, when we use the term "advocate," think of a legal advocate. In the Advocate step, there are many possibilities for the handler, but they all boil down to standing in the gap for the asset. It can occur in micro-situations, like individual conversations, making sure the asset is not excluded, or it could occur in larger, more demanding situations such as helping the asset navigate government programs or trace down critical information.

NEGATIVE EXAMPLES

The negative examples of this step are numerous. It is even pervasive in the disability nomenclature on academic websites, where assets are constantly reminded to be their own advocate. While this holds well-meaning intentions, it breeds the gnawing sense of isolation, as if the asset were the only one in the fight. This ugly sense of isolation leaves the asset exhausted, having to fight tooth and nail for every element of their existence with government agencies, hospitals, and health insurance programs. Then, when it comes to the social life of the assets, they are proverbially out of gas, especially since their attempts at engaging with others in the past were not often reciprocated. This reinforces their feelings of loneliness and isolation.

By launching a disability ministry, churches are attempting to rectify a problem when they notice this pattern of frustration and isolation in the disability community. I am thankful for this. At the same time, what is often accidentally communicated is that to become an advocate or to roll up your sleeves and help, one needs to enroll as an official volunteer in the disability ministry. This unfortunately ends up communicating a kind of unnatural way of caring.

If the only way for the handlers to *gather with* those with a disability is if they become a vital part of the disability ministry, this means the church at large, by implication, is not communicating the same love and care to all. The average church member might reason, "I am kind of drawn toward helping someone with a disability, but I do not think I want to make the huge commitment which the disability ministry is asking for."

This is one of the reasons why the goal of the Five-Step Plan is *not* to set up a disability ministry, but to create a mindset that permeates the entire culture, so the asset does not feel like people are just helping them as a part of their commitment to the disability ministry. The Five-Step Plan is not a specific program but a lifestyle to be adopted by everyone in a particular church, school, or organization.

A specific negative example came up when I (Jason) was interviewing my friend, who I'll call Amber. Amber wanted to go on a trip to Israel and was told it was fully accessible. However, upon arrival, it was a complete disaster. She could not go into any of the places the group was visiting. She could not even physically get out of the hotel or easily get into it. She felt bad because to receive help, some of the group members had to stay behind, which made her feel like a burden.

Later, accompanied by her husband, Amber returned to Israel. She discovered she easily could have visited the various sites and events the group attended if someone had pointed out and advocated for a different route that was right next to where the group went! This anecdote demonstrates the importance of each step and how a few simple inquiries can turn a horrible experience into an enjoyable one for everyone.

Amber's story is but one example. One thing I have noticed on some foreign trips and mission trips is that "the less information given out the better." I think it is seen as having *faith* in the organization or leadership of the trip. But clarifying information lets an asset know if they should attend or not. For example, I am fine if a location or event is genuinely inaccessible. However, one time I was told, like Amber, that a place I wanted to visit was inaccessible. Then one of my friends who went ahead later informed me, "It totally was accessible!"

ADVOCATE AS BRIDGE

Therefore, we not only need people to function as advocates, but we also need to have a better way of communicating accessibility or lack thereof about events, services, and activities. The advocate functions as a constant bridge at this point.

During the Incorporate step, bridge building was only periodic. The Advocate step involves naturally looking out for ways to step out and step in. Advocating is constant bridge building. Is this not what our Savior does for us? Dane Ortlund deftly defines intercession when he notes,

> In general terms it means that a third party comes between two others and makes a case to one on behalf of the other. Think of a parent interceding to a teacher on behalf of a child or an agent interceding to a sports franchise on behalf of an athlete. . . . Intercession applies what the atonement accom-

plished. Christ's present heavenly intercession on our behalf is a reflection of the fullness and victory and completeness of his earthly work, not a reflection of anything lacking in his earthly work. The atonement accomplished our salvation; intercession is the moment-by-moment application of that atoning work.[1]

Advocating can manifest itself in several ways. One of the key elements is sticking up for the asset when they are not even present. For example, you can mention to a larger group that a particular restaurant is inaccessible, but another option might be perfect. In general, the Advocate step might mean the entire group (not just the handler) adopts the mindset of our engagement content. Finally, a key step in this arena is advising when things are under construction. For example, a road, bridge, or walkway may show up on a GPS map as accessible but may in fact currently be inaccessible.

Another key component of Step 5 is ensuring the asset is not left out of conversations. The asset can be excluded from conversations in several ways. One, the group is huddled together, and the asset goes unnoticed because the others are grouped together. Or, perhaps, the group is sometimes physically located where the asset cannot go. This happens when something like furniture is in the way, a table is inaccessible, or a door is not easily opened. Even if the group is situated where an asset can go, oftentimes because of consistent social isolation, the asset does not know how to *break into* the group, especially when the conversation revolves around a topic the asset is not passionate about. I'm not advocating for the group only discussing ideas or events of which the asset is fully aware, but simply making sure the asset can be heard in the conversation.

A positive effect of our Advocate step is it taking some of the burden off the person with a disability. I am not saying advocating solves everything, but it gives the asset a break from having to constantly be on guard, continually having to look for dangerous traps lurking ahead. This works especially well in cooperation with the other five steps.

---

1. Dane Ortlund, *Gentle and Lowly: The Heart of Christ for Sinners and Sufferers* (Wheaton, IL: Crossway, 2020), 79.

For example, a friend named River had consistently shown care and concern for my situation. We first met when she stepped up and noticed I (Jason) needed help removing paper from a printer. Then she helped me finish a massive term paper for a particular class. She also railed against the drama club: while performing a play about people with disabilities, one of the stage props blocked the only accessible entrance to the auditorium. I want you to let the irony of that sink in. In presenting a play intentionally focusing on access for PWDs, we were unable to see it, due to accessibility issues.

My friend Amber, mentioned earlier, had to be physically lifted into this same auditorium because of this same blocked access problem, due to a class she needed to attend while the stage was up for several days. But a key event occurred with River and me. She asked me if I wanted to go to the art museum. One of the most refreshing moments of my life was that I did not have to think about particulars of accessibility. I knew from our honest relationship she had considered these issues. So I just agreed and enjoyed myself. And while I am not too fond of art, I went because she had shown herself to be a faithful friend.

I do not want to draw too fine a point, but this story illustrates the activity does not need to be the greatest event of all time; it just needs to be undertaken together. On a related note, River again demonstrated here her true friendship because, unfortunately, I had failed to charge my power wheelchair before the trip. My chair died once we got to the museum. She had to push me the rest of the way and then had to push me back to my dorm. This demonstrated to me that she exemplified the mindset of Advocate.

Another positive example of advocacy was the men's choir I was a member of, because of the president of the men's choir, John. John visited the church venues where the choirs would perform to ensure accessible entrances. He further organized a group of guys who would be my personal care attendants while on tour. He served as my point person for any difficulties I would encounter. He often developed creative solutions, such as using a block of wood to serve as a ramp onto the stage, or in the most extreme case, organizing a group of strong men to carry my manual wheelchair up into the inaccessible choir loft. I was able to develop friendships with many members of the group and do something I thought would be impossible—spend time with my peers without the awkward barrier of an older personal care attendant. My fellow choirmates received exposure to the life of a person with a disability. It allowed me, for the first time, to benefit from having access to inside jokes. Imagine your whole life being told, "Oh, don't worry, Jason, it's an inside joke—*you* wouldn't understand."

A couple of misconceptions need to be cleared up. Is the advocate a person or a whole group? In some senses, it is both. It starts out as one person, and indeed one person at a time is normally advocating. But eventually the hope of the five steps spreads to others. There emerges a team of support for the asset, so that one person alone is not solely responsible for the success of the entire event, outing, or project.

This is often accomplished through multiple members of a group developing a relationship spurred on by the original handler, so they become handlers themselves. This limits the risk of burnout for the original handler.

As far as practical application of this step, it may sound simple, but really all that needs to be done is to be an advocate. Do it! Show people you care. Connect with them. Connect with the larger group. As you consistently take this step, the mindset of both the group and the asset will shift. Note that in some senses these steps must be sequential, because they build on each other. Handlers cannot incorporate if they have not done research. They cannot advocate if they have not built trust and dependability. In some sense, with every asset you start at point zero since you must build a sense of dependability and trust. The more a handler does it, the easier it becomes. To use a football analogy, every game starts with no score, but the more you practice, and the more plays you master, the easier it becomes to win.

Jesus is your advocate. When you were far from the Father, he offered to bring you near. When you were dead in your sins and trespasses, he made a way for you to live. When you were living under the verdict of guilt, Jesus offered freedom. You were living in darkness; he brought you into the light. You were an orphan, but he adopted you and brought you into his forever family. The Five-Step Plan also serves to describe your salvation. He *noticed* your helpless estate. He *engaged* you by drawing you to himself. It didn't take much *research* for you to discover Jesus was a real person, who died on a cross, and really did rise from the dead. You *incorporated* this truth into your life and placed your faith in Jesus. He is now your *advocate*. "An intercessor stands between two parties; an advocate doesn't simply stand in between the two parties but steps over and joins the one party as he approaches the other."[2]

Jesus advocates for you. Will you now advocate for others?

CONCLUSION

Congratulations! You have made it to the finish line. We have been on a journey together, radically exploring a new way to develop friendships between assets and handlers. Throughout the pages of this final section of the book, we covered the following five steps:

1. *Notice.* The handler notices the environment and recognizes the existence of the asset.
2. *Engage.* The handler seeks out the asset and connects with them, asking questions, learning about likes, dislikes, and limitations.
3. *Research.* The handler takes the information from engaging and applies it either passively, noting areas as they live their lives; or actively, planning where the asset would be able to go and would enjoy going.
4. *Incorporate.* The handler becomes a bridge between the asset and the larger group, where joint activities are consistently undertaken that can be enjoyed by all. We also discussed the importance of the handler getting group buy-in for the activity and that doing small activities consistently builds trust with the asset.
5. *Advocate.* The handler serves as a consistent bridge for the asset, mediating for the asset in group discussions, making sure that access *remains* accessible, and potentially doing the legwork of wrestling with the government and other agencies.

---

2. Ortlund, *Gentle and Lowly*, 8.

Taken together, these five steps help create genuine friendship between the two and remove the psychological barriers ingrained within the asset of inadequacy, isolation, and genuine feelings of being unloved and unwanted.

A key component of the Five-Step Plan versus standard disability ministry is that the focus of this plan is individual. As explained, the importance of this is paramount because no disability affects two people in the same way. Therefore, to be effective the help and support needs to be tailored to the individual. Being person-based serves another practical effect, demonstrating the handler genuinely cares for the asset, not because they are part of a program but, rather, simply because they bear the image of God. While Paul and I were doing research for this book, we discovered there was something called the "Five Steps of Awareness." The steps enumerated in this thought were not what one should *do*, but where one is in their *mindset* regarding people with disabilities. While this look at awareness serves to be helpful, again this does not solve the problem of actually getting to your goal.

The intended effects of the Five-Step Plan are to create a sense of being cared for within the asset and a genuine understanding of sacrificial love on the part of the handler. This can take an immense amount of time depending on the trauma the asset has taken on over the years. Related to this, the focus of the five steps should not be on reaching the largest number of people possible (a problem that we sometimes have in the evangelical subculture of the United States), but rather to focus on quality versus quantity, care over numbers.

Jesus himself only had twelve disciples, and they were able to impact the entire Roman world in just one generation. God often does more with a few than he does with many. Finally, the ultimate intended result of the Five-Step Plan is genuine *friendship*, not just presence. This results from a change in mindset on the part of the handler. The handler begins to see and proactively think of the needs of potential assets, not just their own current asset involvement. I have also noticed those who have exposure to assets either through friendship or family are most often the ones who treat other assets with authentic, genuine care. One of the goals of this book, therefore, was to create that first experience. We hope and pray this vision casting and the detailed explanation of the Five-Step Plan has served you well.

Our hope is for the Five-Step Plan to spread organically throughout churches and organizations. Ideally, we desire the entire church to share this mindset, so the burden of help would not fall on one handler alone. This would also help potential handlers so that, as their mindset grows, they will be able to serve as better witnesses of Jesus Christ. The proximity to the asset will also allow the asset to minister to them, since oftentimes assets, because they are ignored, cannot fully utilize their specific spiritual gifts.

Since our emphasis is on an individual, bottom-up approach, this book is for everyone—perhaps mostly those of you who are not involved in a disability ministry, those of you who never really considered you could be so important to a person with a disability. Because pastors have a unique opportunity of influencing their congregation, we implore pastors reading this to implement these steps. This book is for everyone to apply. In some sense, everyone can benefit from having the five steps applied to them, because we all at one time or another have felt isolated and broken.

Before we end this book, we would like to leave you with one positive example of a church that is performing the five steps well. One of the pleasant recent developments in my life (Jason) has been my moving to Missouri and finding Raintree Community Church. This church exemplifies the five steps. The members constantly look to make paths accessible and even apologized that they have not yet installed an automatic door opener to the bathroom door.

One event, however, stands out in my mind the most. In my current house, I like to spend time in the basement because it has more space. There is one problem, however. There is no path to the basement door, so the ground is difficult to traverse when it is muddy or snowy. I briefly mentioned this in a men's Bible study. A few days later, one of the men approached my mother for more information. A few days after that, he discussed how he reached out to many different agencies, and he gave us a plan for forming a sidewalk. The following day, he brought a friend to measure the area to see how much material was needed. This was a Godsend, because when we had reached out to agencies, we could not reach anyone. Furthermore, we had been completely unaware that this particular agency even offered home modifications.

I tell this story to note I had only known this man for a few weeks, but he went through the full range of the Five-Step Plan. The minor difference was his focus was not social inclusion, such as we have focused on, but on physical help. This served as an encouragement, because as you take these steps, like this man you may find yourself doing them with greater ease and speed.

Another note about this specific church. They do not have a disability ministry. Their care for assets is organic. Part of me wants to call them the "Five-Step Church." What is the reason for this genuine care and awareness? Or the reason there are multiple people with disabilities who stay there? The pastor. Not only does he have a son with severe ADHD, but he has a brother with cerebral palsy. Because of him, this mindset has trickled down to every part of the church. It shows that disability ministries are not always required in order to undertake ministry to people with disabilities. All that is needed is a mindset shift. It is our hope that, as you're reading this book, this new mindset can trickle down to churches or wherever you serve, and we can, together, create a more positive and impactful church and Christian culture where people with disabilities are seen as assets and not just thorns in the side or boxes to be checked.

Interestingly, Raintree Community Church is not a large megachurch with millions of dollars at its disposal, but it is able to do something that can't be purchased: it demonstrates Christlikeness, which is priceless.

This mindset is nothing new for the church at large. It was a common mindset for churches in the first century and Middle Ages, where they would care for the sick and dying, who might typically be avoided. It is this approach of the church, demonstrating their genuine care, which has led many in secular society to join them.

We pray for a new awakening in churches today. What small part might you and I play in the redemptive story God is currently writing? Let each of us work toward the full inclusion of people with disabilities as we help build the beloved community. Let each of us pray about reaching out and building a friendship with a person with a disability. In this way we can help in building up the one body while relying upon the empowering of the one Spirit.

APPENDIX 1

The Glorified Body and What It Reveals About God's View on Disability

There are several places in Scripture where the glorified body is mentioned. In 1 Corinthians 15, it is referred to as a spiritual body juxtaposed with the natural body, which enables, according to Paul, the inheritance and entrance into the eternal state. Christ is also seen to be the firstfruits and the model of our resurrection. Two elements here are significant. First, we note that firstfruits imply more is coming and more of the same kind. Therefore, we can look to Jesus's body as a model. We know after the resurrection he was able to physically interact with material things, like food (Luke 24:42–43), and people were able to touch and feel him (Luke 24:39), clearly establishing that he was corporeal and not incorporeal. After the resurrection Jesus was not a ghost. These components lead us to believe the glorified body will be a physical body that is Spirit-empowered.

Second, in the eternal state there will be no sin. Therefore, there will be no sickness, death, crying, or pain. This is seen in the declarations about the millennium (Isa. 33:24; Rev. 21:4). A point often overlooked in these discussions is the fact we are all suffering from the effects of the sin curse. As everyone gets older, they have trouble seeing, hearing, walking, and even thinking. Each of us experiences entropy. Because of the effects of sin, we are all in some sense marching toward a state of degradation and disability (2 Cor. 4:16). This is one of the reasons why one of the groups of people I (Jason) enjoy spending time with is the older generation—not just because they are more mature than my peers, but because we can sympathize and commiserate with each other's difficulties. In the eternal state and millennial kingdom, however, this decaying process is not only stopped but miraculously reversed.

This insight into the end state of Christians, if you will, shows us we were always meant to be physical beings. Physicality is not evil, contrary to what some mystery religions like the Gnostics supposed. This also shows disability is a direct result of sin being in the world, like any other sickness and difficulty. "As he passed by, he saw a man blind from birth. And his disciples asked him, 'Rabbi, who sinned, this man or his parents, that he was born blind?' Jesus answered, 'It was not that this man sinned, or his parents, but that the works of God might be displayed in him'" (John 9:1–3). The question, therefore, of why God does not currently heal everyone is akin to the ancient Israelite struggle of judgment not occurring immediately. God will restore and heal everyone in his own time, in the eternal state.

For some with disabilities, including myself, a body free from pain and physical impairment is difficult to imagine, especially if our current state is the only body we have ever known. In my case, it is almost impossible for me to imagine being able to run, swim, wrestle, and so on. In fact, one thing I look forward to immensely is finally being able to kneel in front of God's throne. The fact that I am not currently able to kneel in prayer fills me with a twinge of sadness. But I remind myself this is only temporary.

I know some people who find their identity in their disability community so much so that total healing would isolate them from their friends and everyone they know. Everyone has the potential to struggle with where their identity truly lies, whether they have a disability or not. Anyone can place their identity in anything—their intelligence, their job, their personality. As hard as it is, however, we need to strive to place our importance and our worth in what Jesus labeled us—a child of God. Having this mindset helps remove the fear of disconnection. Regardless, though, in the eternal state, no one will have a disability, so there will not even be a possibility for micro-identities. According to the book of Revelation, it seems that one of the major points is every division we can think of—tribes, tongues, languages, nations–are all suspended as we come together for one glorious purpose while the individual elements remain distinct (Rev. 7:9). This is a beautiful example of unity within diversity. It will be an experience of oneness without sameness. In an indirect way, this shows us God's ultimate desire is for his heterogeneous children to strive together to accomplish his good purpose.

God always intended humans to be both spiritual and physical—the physical body is not evil. We have witnessed the existence of disability in the world because of the impact of sin, causing our bodies to degrade. This process will be reversed in our glorified bodies. This demonstrates not only that we are more than the sum of our disability, but also that we will be free of all of life's difficulties and pains to enjoy unimpeded access to God and God's people forever, fulfilling our ultimate design.

APPENDIX 2

The Imago Dei *and Its Impact on People with Disabilities*

All human beings possess what theologians have often called the imago Dei, or "image of God." This theological concept originates from Genesis 1:26. There has been considerable scholastic debate over what extent the *imago Dei* still exists in human beings because of the fall or what elements of humanity constitute the *imago Dei*. While we may never have a full understanding of what the *imago Dei* is, it is clear what some of its influences are if we look at the animal kingdom.

Human beings can do things animals cannot. We can plan and think about the future instead of just solely relying on instinct. We also create and innovate. We can perceive things outside of our immediate situation and social group. We can love and care for others. While sin affected the full core of our beings, it did not remove the *imago Dei* completely. This is seen in God's interchange with Noah about the appropriate use of divine punishment, where God states if any person murders another, they themselves must be killed (Gen. 9:6). The grounding here is because man was made in God's image. This shows that despite what the fall and sin have done to humanity, we continue to bear the *imago Dei*.

Because of this, people with disabilities also possess the very same *imago Dei*, which gives them immense value. In the past, PWDs have sometimes been seen as second-class citizens. I have also observed the other side, where while not denying the value of PWDs, they have sometimes been treated as though they were an impediment to everyone. This is directly opposed to Jesus's own actions. Instead of shunning and treating the blind, paralyzed, and the deaf as people to be ignored, he engaged them and often healed them.

If we are to follow Christ as Christians, we need to strive to act as Christ. This includes not just mentally affirming that PWDs are made in the *imago Dei*, but putting that theological thought into action, welcoming them and engaging with them, attempting to perform the Five-Step Plan, for example. If we do this, we not only imitate Christ, but we practically affirm that the love we have for the person with a disability is not just a hollow platitude, but is rooted in genuine action.

APPENDIX 3

The Difficulties of a Person with a Disability Serving in a Church and a Possible Solution

The church in America has a problem: numbers reign supreme. If someone does not fit into the church's preestablished schema of ministries, they are regularly not given opportunities to serve and engage. The type of people churches often look for are either charismatic entertainers or grunt laborers. Regularly in these types of churches, newcomers must pay their dues by doing manual labor for an indeterminate amount of time until they are elevated to another position. This not only prevents people from using their individual gifting, but also is a major roadblock to people with disabilities. Often what is communicated in many churches is that PWDs are only objects to be served—or on the other hand, people to be held up on a pedestal like motivational speakers who climbed Mount Everest. But this is counter to the *imago Dei* and the goal of unity in Christ's body.

According to 1 Corinthians, every part of the body must work together. Parts that are not seen as worthy of honor are treated with special honor (1 Cor. 12:21–26). All of us are meant to work together in service. Practically, this means removing the *ladder rung* service philosophy, where to get what is considered "higher," more showy ministries like teaching or leading, one must first engage in service work like physically cleaning a building or setting up chairs. While this plan may work for most people, for people with disabilities it often inhibits us from ever entering into service. Since often we cannot engage in physical grunt tasks, we do not enter the *pay-your-dues* cycle, which means we are rarely given opportunities.

At least in my (Jason's) experience when I have proactively sought out leadership for service opportunities, church leaders have either shrugged and pushed me away, or given me a platitude of "We will find something for you," which often failed to materialize. To combat this, churches can create a one-on-one mentoring and discipleship program to plug people into service opportunities. While this approach is especially helpful for those struggling with a disability, it is ideally helpful for everyone. In this one-on-one discipleship strategy, the person discipling will be able to effectively attest to the quality and character of the person they are working with, gradually giving them increased responsibility and providing them with feedback. This will also help many churches avoid the problem of inadvertently communicating that only certain types of people are wanted to serve at that church, namely extroverted musicians or people who want to work in children's ministry, because often those are the ministries that continually seek volunteers.

In some ways, readers might notice that my approach to correcting this deficiency in the church mirrors our book's Five-Step Plan. It requires someone to work with, support, and go to bat for the person with disabilities. For a person with disabilities to get an opportunity to serve, often someone else must plead their case before the church leaders. There are churches—few, but some still exist—that have not had this pay-your-dues philosophy. In these churches, I was observed as committed and involved in the church and this is what immediately opened the door for me to serve and co-lead several Bible studies. When I talked with the pastor of one of these churches about his philosophy, he said he wanted to use my giftings. He had no expectation that I would lift boxes or restock the coffee station. Since each of us is given a spiritual gift for the advancement of the body, it is best for the church at large to help people become involved in the ministry where their spiritual gift fits best. Many churches do spiritual gift inventories, which is a great first step.

But I observed that the ball often gets dropped after that step. There is really no help in plugging in and having opportunities presented on a regular basis. A person often struggles to plug themselves into the ministries where they would fit. To reiterate, discipleship is needed across the board in our churches, but particularly for PWDs because we have the hardest time connecting to the broader community since we often cannot perform the same tasks as others. My hope is that if these suggestions of discipleship and individual service tailoring are executed, people with disabilities will be able to bring their individual gifts and therefore strengthen their local church body as a whole.

Since Christians are intended to use their gifts to mutually edify one another, when one is prevented from doing so the whole body suffers. It is interesting that sometimes people's disabilities help them to serve more effectively. I knew a person who was mentally impaired, and because he had little social inhibition he could easily and fearlessly proclaim the gospel. Now, he could not easily answer questions from the people he was talking to, but his unrestrained boldness was something we can all learn from and something that can serve as an encouragement to us. How can you help others, especially PWDs, use their gifts for the building up of the body?

APPENDIX 4
Fifty Potential Objections

NOTICE

1. I am busy; it's not my job to go around all day noticing people.
We all make time for what we consider important. Oftentimes we are not as busy as we think we are. I would encourage you to think about what Jesus would do. According to the Gospels, it seems he would regularly take a detour to notice people.

2. I rarely notice anyone; I am a task person.
In a way, this objection betrays the quasi-universality of the five steps, meaning you should notice anyone who is excluded or isolated. Regarding this objection, I would urge you to challenge yourself to be more intentional about observing your surroundings. Being more observant could even help you finish your tasks more efficiently.

3. I have looked; there are no people with disabilities around me.
In very rare cases, there are no people with disabilities in our spheres. Oftentimes, however, we may simply be unaware. In this case, there are several things I would suggest. One, practice the Notice step on anyone who seems lonely or isolated. Two, intentionally seek out those with disabilities at places such as rehab hospitals and community centers. You may find that once you find and interact with one person, you will find it easier to locate people with disabilities in your normal sphere, like when you notice something for the first time and then start seeing it everywhere.

4. Sometimes I notice someone, but I am not sure if they are disabled.
Notice is not dependent on whether someone has a disability. In fact, the very point of Notice is to set the stage for Engage, where you would gain information about the person. To put it simply, you could just ask them! But even if they do not have a disability, if they are isolated and alone, they could probably use a friend.

5. *I am married. I am not going to be looking at (noticing) random men/women. This will make my spouse uncomfortable.*

First things first, you should have a discussion with your spouse explaining what you intend to do. Maybe even share this book with them. If you clearly explain your intentions, your spouse most likely will not be uncomfortable. As a general note, there is a difference between looking and staring. People look at each other all the time, or we would run into each other. It's natural to look. You and your spouse could also Notice them and talk to them together. It could be a joint action. If you are both looking, you can help each other notice things that the other misses.

6. *I feel like if I set about noticing people, they will think I am staring at them.*

Often, this concern comes from a place of being too self-conscious. You don't need to thoroughly study a person to notice them. It could just be a simple, quick glance. The goal of noticing is to note those people who are not engaged in the group, who are isolated, whether they have a disability or not.

7. *I already know some people with disabilities and have some friends with disabilities; I do not feel I need to notice any more people with disabilities.*

I'm glad you have some friends with disabilities. But is that how you treat everyone, even those without disabilities? That you have enough friends and do not need anyone else? You can always make another friend. While you may not need a friend, that person with a disability does.

8. *I am currently working on a very important project with an upcoming deadline; I will try to notice people next summer when I have more time.*

Life always gets busy. If you want, you can always find a new excuse or a new activity to occupy yourself. My advice would be to not put it off. Do *something*. At least start down the path.

9. I am afraid if I begin taking an active notice of all the people with disabilities around me, I will get discouraged or even depressed.

Start small. You do not have to try to notice every single person. Just notice one and start there. It might also help to do some introspection to see why you are worried about being depressed. You may find in this step that you experience the opposite of being depressed. Serving often produces joy.

10. I see everyone the same.

In one sense it is true that we are all the same in that we are all created in the image of God. In another, we have differences and strengths and weaknesses. But Notice is not about noticing differences or even similarities. It's primarily about noticing people who are on the fringes of the group. We are specifically focusing on people with disabilities.

ENGAGE

11. Engaging someone is awkward.

Just do it! Do you not usually talk to anyone new? How else are you supposed to create friendships?

12. I am afraid if I engage someone, they will tell me to mind my own business.

This reaction you are worried about is very rare, especially because people with disabilities are often alone and hungry for friendship. Even if this is their response, however, you have at least done what you could. It is their choice how they respond.

13. If I engage someone, they will probably begin taking advantage of me.

This is a legitimate concern and requires an honest conversation as the relationship develops. This issue mainly comes into play with Incorporate and Advocate. The best solution to this is to try to create a network of other advocates to share the load. This is important to do because each person has their limits, no matter how much they want to help.

14. *If I am engaging with a minor, their parents could yell at me or contact the authorities.*

Use common sense. Engage with them in public spaces where other people are present. Maybe talk to the parents beforehand and clarify your intentions. Most parents will be overjoyed to have someone talking to their child normally. Instead of being mad and yelling at you, they will likely be relieved and thankful. Kids with disabilities often do not have friends because they cannot engage in "normal" kid activities.

15. *I do not know how to engage someone with a disability; what would I even say?*

Follow the suggestions mentioned in this book. In general, ask questions as to what they like, what they do not like. Even ask them directly about their disability. As mentioned earlier in this book, most of the time people with disabilities not only are okay with you asking about their disability, but are overjoyed to tell you about it because this is a huge part of their life that you are taking an interest in. Plus, in asking about their disability, you are at least being honest about the questions they most likely know you are thinking and you are showing you have the courage to ask.

16. *I am afraid I will blurt out something offensive if I engage, so I just try to smile.*

While I understand the fear, even if you blurt out something offensive, it's better than not doing anything. The chances that you say something offensive are very small. For example, my coauthor, Paul, during the initial stages of writing, did not use person-first language (e.g., "person with a disability" vs. "disabled person") very much, which some in the disabled community might take issue with, and I personally do not prefer. However, these word choices did not stop me from pursuing a friendship with him because I was happy to have a friend. I did not care if he did not say all the right things every single time. Especially nowadays, what often offends one person does not offend another, so open dialogue is the key and the willingness to ask for understanding and forgiveness.

17. What if I say something and the person with the disability takes it the wrong way?

Like the previous objection, open dialogue is the key on both sides. It might be helpful for you as the handler to mention to the asset that if anything offends them or they are confused about what you might have meant, to ask for clarification just as you would in any conversation. A good practice could be the therapeutic of "what I heard you say was . . . ".

18. I am afraid if I engage, I will encounter some specific medical condition the person with the disability has.

There are several solutions to this objection. Most physical disabilities are not contagious. As far as having to help with specific medical concerns, you should be open and honest as to what you are comfortable with and be willing to listen to the asset's medical difficulties. In fact, in some cases, often what the asset may need is somebody to just observe them and call 911 or rush them to the hospital if something happens. For instance, I have a medical pump; if it fails, I go into severe withdrawal symptoms. I have told several of my friends of these symptoms and what to do in that case, which mainly centers around them taking me to the doctor's office as quickly as possible.

19. I would engage more often but my spouse tells me to "mind my own business."

My suggestion would be to give your spouse this book. Affirm to them that engaging is what Jesus did. We are all thankful that Jesus did not "mind his own business."

20. I would engage more often but I already have three friends who each have their own disability.

One needs to be aware of the time they can give, but if you do not have time to engage to the same degree with everyone, be honest with it and upfront. But I would encourage you to at least do some elements of Engage. If you are honest about your own limitations, it may still help the asset see how much you care. A quick solution would be to invite them into conversations with your other friends. This would allow you to "save time," but make a space for the new person to feel included and loved.

RESEARCH

21. If I do not have time to engage, I do not have time to research; I work forty hours per week.

You may not have the ability to do active research, where you purposely seek out locations for activities and go through dry runs, which takes more time. But regardless of how busy you are, you can always do passive research. Passive research is noticing as you go through life what areas are accessible and what areas are not. This is not an additional time commitment; it just requires being observant. There is a reason Engage comes before Research, however. The information gained from the Engage step fuels Research, since each person's disability affects them differently. If you do not engage with a particular person, it renders the Research step almost impossible beyond gathering general information and awareness. For example, you may note if a building has ramps or an elevator, but not whether a particular person's wheelchair will fit into the elevator or through a door.

22. When you say "research," do you mean doing scientific studies?

No. When we say "research," we mean field research or practical research, meaning that you as the handler, after gaining a rudimentary understanding of the asset's limitations, observe or research what areas might be accessible or inaccessible to them. The most effective way to do this is to go to the location, as simply calling and asking questions is not a guarantee that the place is accessible. The more effort you put into research, the greater the asset will trust that you genuinely care about them.

23. I can go out and do research, but I do not know if I am helping my friend with a disability or not.

The Research step starts with information from Engage. So you should know the individual person's limitations and what they like and dislike. If you know what they like and dislike and what their limitations are, then you are helping, even if you discover the location you were researching is not accessible because you know it is not a possibility for that individual. With Research you are helping the asset because you are helping expand the possibility of activities they can do. Oftentimes we assets are trapped in a rut, unable to experience new things in life because we do not have the abilities to confirm their possibility. Whenever we have tried, we have been met with insurmountable obstacles. That is why we need a handler to help, someone who is not burdened with a physical disability and has the freedom to be our "boots on the ground." If you are not sure, ask assets if they would enjoy the activity you are considering or if they have tried it before.

24. If I am being honest with myself, I guess I do not care enough to go and do all this advance work; perhaps someone who is closer to my friend can do this.

Sometimes people with disabilities do not have anyone else. Or if they do, they are often focused on maintaining what is necessary for a person to live. Therefore, they don't have the time or energy to devote to researching fun activities.

25. Shouldn't the family of the person with disabilities be doing this research?

As in the answer to the previous objection, often the family is busy with all the necessary elements of life. And there are some cases in which the family is not present. For example, when I went to my undergrad school, none of my family was there. One of the points of this step is for the asset to see how much the handler cares. The firsthand experience of research can help the handler be more effective in the Incorporate and the Advocate stages.

26. I just met my new friend who has a disability; I need to wait for a year or two so I can really get to know their likes and dislikes.

Research can and should be an ongoing dialogue. The Research step allows you to gain more information which in turn allows you to ask questions of the asset. Both Engage and Research feed into each other if done well. If you bring the asset in on this conversation, this will show them you care because you are willing to enter their world.

27. *If I undertake research for the five friends with disabilities I have, I will turn research into a full-time job!*

I understand your time concern. However, there are several possibilities you can implement. One, you can utilize passive research. This does not take nearly as much time. Another possibility is that your friends may have similar disabilities. For instance, they may all use power wheelchairs for mobility. In that case, researching one location would be fine. If they have different disabilities, you could keep that in mind when you are researching a certain location, for example, noting where the elevators are, knowing whether a sign language interpreter is available, and so on and so forth. Finally, there is a real possibility that even if these five friends of yours have similar disabilities, they may have different interests. While I have advocated that the activities should be something they and the group enjoy, oftentimes assets will simply go to an activity just to be with people, not necessarily because they enjoy it. For instance, I do not like art museums at all. I find them incredibly boring. But when my friend Sandi was in town and asked me if I wanted to go to see the Van Gogh exhibit, I said yes—not because I like art, but because I enjoy her company and I knew she enjoyed art. And given our prior relationship, I knew she would ensure that it would be entirely accessible.

28. *This research is expensive—I cannot drive all over town scouting out routes and touring buildings!*

It does not have to be expensive. You just find one or two locations the asset might enjoy. Even then, this can be done via passive research which will not cost anything at all except time.

29. *We live in a small town; there is no real research to be done.*

Research is even more crucial in a small town! Often small towns are less equipped for people with disabilities. It may take more work or more planning or thinking outside the box—for instance, seeing if a ramp would work on an entrance or if there is a nonconventional entrance. One time when the elevator broke in a movie theater, I had to go through the loading dock and use that elevator. And the elevator I used in the bookstore on my undergraduate campus was mainly used for merchandise movement.

30. *My friend has a severe cognitive disability, so I think any activity we undertake should be fine.*

While cognitive disabilities are not the focus of this book, I do believe that research for a person with a cognitive disability could be even more crucial and difficult. For instance, are they sensitive to crowds or noises? Flashing lights? Is the activity something they would enjoy? What activity would best fit them and the group? What group would be a good match for them? If their mental age is drastically lower than their chronological age, maybe an activity for children would better fit them. But all this should be done in dialogue with the individual person. Some people I know with cognitive disabilities still desire adult activities.

INCORPORATE

31. *I wanted to undertake this activity, and my friend with a disability did also, but our larger friend group had little interest.*

There are several possibilities. One, you and your friend can do the activity, just the two of you, and search for an activity for later that everyone would enjoy. Two, you can find the people in the group who would like to do that activity and do it with them as well. For Incorporate, not everyone in the larger group needs to be present, but it is ideal that it would be more than just the single handler and asset for several reasons: This gives other people the opportunity of exposure which can potentially create new handlers, lessening the burden on the first. It can also help reinforce the fact that the first handler wants to do the activity.

32. *I think my friend with a disability can undertake this activity, but they keep insisting they cannot. I think they need to stretch a little bit and step out in faith.*

I would ask them why they do not believe they can do the activity and then try to see if you can account for those objections. Make sure you are listening to their concerns. If there are tangible objections, they should be accounted for. What really makes Incorporate effective, though, is if the handler can predict what the objections would be and comes to the asset mentioning the potential objections and their solutions. This will help the asset see how genuine the handler's concern for them is. It might also be helpful to start smaller because that builds the asset's confidence that you would help them.

33. *I feel like I've lost some of my own identity because I'm always doing what my friend with a disability wants to do.*

This is a genuine concern and something we are trying to avoid with Incorporate. You may get burned out. The asset may feel you are only doing this to check a box. And they may believe the only reason you are doing this is out of pity. That is why Incorporate focuses on *mutually* enjoyable activities and doing them regularly, so the assets can clearly see they are not being a burden to you or the group. In fact, the fear of being a burden to the group or limiting their fun is one of the major reasons why I regularly have withdrawn from social activities. I viewed myself constantly as a buzzkill, someone who would just reduce the maximum amount of fun the group would have and therefore it would be better for me not to be there. This sentiment of the greater good was regularly communicated, most poignantly by a dormitory resident assistant who directly said, "I have fifty guys on this floor—I can't worry about one." I've also found this fear to be well founded when I directly asked one of my few friends on the floor, and he affirmed that the guys did see me as someone who would ruin their fun.

34. *I feel like all we ever do is church-related activities.*

This sentiment can be completely accurate and is why Research is important. The Research step allows the potential of exploring new activities or locations. Assets want to be in the community if they can.

35. *The asset I am helping has a degenerative condition, so I never know if they will be able to be involved in these activities.*

With a degenerative condition, constant dialogue is even more important. In addition to that, you can help the asset be realistic about what they can do currently. They will need the friendship even more as they struggle to constantly readjust. Regarding their involvement in activities, plan for what they can do now. With a degenerative condition, you do not know what is going to happen. You can only plan for now. Help them squeeze as much as they can out of life.

36. *I do not have access to a disability-equipped vehicle, so I do not know what to do.*

Depending on your location, there are several options. Sometimes a vehicle is not needed if you live in a small area. Other times public transportation helps. Occasionally there are some accessible taxis as well. Sometimes community centers or similar places have accessible vehicles. The other possibility is that a church could pursue acquiring an accessible vehicle or ask for one to be donated. The last two wheelchair vans I have had were donated to us, so it never hurts to ask. You could also purchase a used van from a nonprofit, like Make a Wish. It is always worth a dialogue with the asset because they may have figured out ways of transportation themselves. A normal vehicle can be used sometimes. For example, if someone uses a wheelchair, perhaps they could use their manual wheelchair and transfer into a regular seat and stow the manual wheelchair in the trunk. The assets themselves may have a wheelchair-accessible vehicle but may need someone to drive.

37. *Sometimes I feel like I am doing all this incorporating just to check off a box.*

Reflect on why you are doing this. Why do you feel like you are checking off a box? Do you feel like you are not in the proper headspace? Go back to Engage. Do you not enjoy the activities? Try to find activities you both enjoy or a more compatible friend for the asset. If you feel that it is something that might correct itself over time, be involved and get more exposure. Sometimes you just need experience. You may feel like you are checking off a box now, but it may grow into something more. You may not initially like the person, but a friendship can develop. It is better to do something and be imperfect than to worry about being perfect and not doing anything. Go back to Engage. Recognize that you do not have to pursue friendship with every asset you meet. Some people just do not click. In that circumstance, sometimes the best thing you can do is help the asset find a person they would mesh better with. For example, if you know from Engage that the asset likes musicals, but you cannot stand them, you can help them connect to a friend of yours who likes musicals as well. You can be a liaison to find more compatible friends for the asset.

38. Sometimes I feel like my friend with a disability should be transitioning to independence by now.

The amount of independence a person with a disability can achieve varies from person to person. Even when a person with a disability strives for independence, often they can never be fully independent, as much as they would like. For instance, I could be considered independent, but I still require someone to get me up in the morning and assist me in getting ready for the day . . . and I always will. I will always require someone to help make meals and perform other daily tasks as well as handle transportation issues. There are some elements in my life that, as much as I want to, I will never be able to do on my own. It is possible that you could have a conversation with the asset and see if they have any fears about being independent or if there is any way you can help them become more independent. It should be obvious, but this is not a day-one conversation. This is after trust is built and genuine care is consistently shown. In fact, as you spend time with the asset, you may either (1) realize a potential solution they never thought of, or (2) realize your initial feelings of their needing independence in those areas are not realistic.

39. Helen Keller and Joni Eareckson Tada seemed to do fine on their own. I don't think they needed a team of people assisting them.

We need to first acknowledge that Helen Keller specifically had a very patient teacher, Anne Sullivan, to help her work through the difficulties of her disability. Joni Eareckson Tada has written that her husband, Ken, was extremely helpful in her life after her diving accident. At this point, she likely has numerous people helping her behind the scenes. Just because we do not see the network does not mean it is not there. In fact, these two people remind us that it was their network that allowed them to make such a massive impact. Imagine if Helen Keller did not have Anne Sullivan to teach her and to provide continued care.

40. Sometimes I feel like my friend with a disability is putting too much trust in me and not trying to do things on their own.

This objection seems very similar to objection 32. First off, it is great that they trust you! In some sense, you may be allowing them to do activities that they would not be able to do by themselves. As in the response to objection 32, take a step back and observe whether they would be able to do the things you think they could do on their own. It is quite possible you could help them brainstorm creative solutions. Again, you could simply ask them. Say something to the effect of, "Do you want to try doing X? I believe you could do it." Or, "What are your concerns about doing X?"

ADVOCATE

41. I am tired of always being the one to fight for my asset; can we rotate this role among our friend group?

First off, in some senses, I am glad you are getting tired of fighting for them because that gives you a small taste of what the asset must go through. To answer your specific question, yes, it is possible to rotate this role among many others. That is one of the benefits of the Incorporate step. While you may take a step back from actively advocating, though, the mindset never stops. The responsibility can be shared, but it should not be handled like passing off a chore that no one wants to do.

42. I believe the Holy Spirit is our advocate; I am afraid I might mess up and lead my friend with a disability down the wrong road in life.

The Holy Spirit is our advocate to God and our assistant in sanctification. However, when we use the term "advocate," we are not specifically talking about advising their spiritual journey. The Advocate step is mainly centered around sticking up for the asset in the broader community. If you mess up, the Holy Spirit can course-correct.

43. I keep advocating for my asset and me to attend church, but she always has an excuse. Should I drop this friend and look for a new project to work on?

First and foremost, what we are looking for is genuine friendship, not a "project" for evangelism. Whether or not the asset comes to church would be irrelevant in one sense. On the other hand, are their excuses legitimate? Have you ensured that there is an accessible way? Have you continually proven yourself in the small things to be someone who could be relied upon? Again, the Advocate step is centered around helping the assets and standing up for them, not accomplishing a project.

44. Can I do something crazy like taking my asset skydiving or water-skiing?

Yes! It just requires planning and making sure all the necessary adaptive equipment is available. It is a lot more work, but it is possible. Doing something crazy like that, however, will require a lot of trust on the part of the asset. So I would suggest starting small and doing little things often to build the asset's confidence. Doing little things even applies to inviting someone to a somewhat bigger event like a weekend retreat. For instance, when I was in a college group, I was practically ignored by everyone there. They were going on a summer retreat, and the pastor mentioned he would like me to attend and would make it work. I thought about the possibility for a while and eventually decided that I did not want to go because I would likely be ignored there too—and that would happen after a lot more effort on my part to arrange the logistics, since no one was advocating for me at the time. This is an important thing to keep in mind, because often assets' minds go into the framework of risk versus reward.

45. What if I advocate for an activity and my asset gets injured? I fear a lawsuit.

One, at the Advocate stage you are not advocating for an activity. It is more that you are advocating for the asset's inclusion and needs. Activities fall more under the purview of Incorporate. However, for the question at hand, lawsuits are a serious concern in this society, especially when we have a plethora of injury lawyers. If you are worried about the asset being injured, you could do less risky activities like going to a museum or concert or sporting event or movie. As things progress, if both of you want to do something riskier, there should be an understanding, perhaps written, that they will not sue you should the worst happen. But this is further down the road. In general, you should not be asking an asset to sign a waiver on your first meeting. Also, if there is a genuine friendship, the chances that they would sue you are very low. It would be far more likely for them to sue the person or company in charge of the activity.

46. How long do we advocate for? Three or four years? After this time do I switch to a new asset?

Advocating is a lifelong process, as this friendship should be lifelong. It is not a momentary experience and then you move on. Now, there is always the possibility that one of you would move and would maybe suspend the advocating state naturally, but, in general, you should not approach advocating with a timestamp. Like the Research and Engage steps, it is also possible to advocate for multiple assets at once, especially if they have similar physical concerns like ramp access or are involved in the same general community group. You can advocate for several assets simultaneously.

47. I am simply not trained for this type of advocacy. I feel I need to get a degree or certificate first. This is much more than the friendship I signed up for!

You do not need a specified degree or certificate. In fact, sometimes purely hypothetical constructs with no practical experience can be counterproductive, especially since many of the models in disability ministry are macro-focused instead of micro-focused. All you essentially need is to be willing to listen and have genuine care and concern. The worry about it being more than the friendship you signed up for is somewhat valid. This honestly is a lot of work. But it is what Jesus did, so if you say that you want to be like Jesus, do it! It's important to remember, however, that you do not have to "save the world." You must be with one person at a time, like the famous parable of the starfish on the beach. You can try to help one!

48. There are so many disability ministries out there. Tell me again why I am the one doing this?

Yes, there are many disability ministries out there. However, most disability ministries are focused on a top-down approach, generally lumping people with disabilities together in one group and not focusing on the individual. While these disability ministries can serve very positive functions, they do not generate, by themselves, authentic friendship. The main reason why you are doing this is to create authentic friendship and to show the asset they are valued and loved. Before I had people practically acting these steps out in my life, I really wondered how God could love someone like me who was weak, broken, and unwanted. I viewed myself as a thorn in everyone's side. I regularly had the mindset from *It's a Wonderful Life*—it would be better if I had not been born.

49. Shouldn't my friend's family be advocating for him? I'm not a family member.

The friend's family are probably advocating for him. However, they are probably unable to advocate in the same areas you are. It is much more effective when a member of the group advocates as opposed to parents and adults. Plus, advocating shows your genuine care for the asset and your willingness to go the extra mile. The fact you are not a family member highlights this reality, because family members are supposed to help each other. When you advocate, it shows you are choosing to help not under an obligation, but out of true care and friendship. This demonstrates true friendship.

50. I am starting to get discouraged with this whole project. It seems we never get any "buy-in" from our larger friend group. It is almost impossible to find an activity that everyone wants to get involved with.

Again, this concern is mostly centered in the Incorporate stage. As far as this is concerned, though, there are two possibilities. One, consider finding the few in the group who want to do the activity. Not everyone has to be involved or present. Sometimes this would be unfeasible based on the number of people. The other possibility is trying to find a different friend group either by seeing if there is another person who meshes better with the asset or, if you desire to do the activity as well, by finding a new friend group for the both of you that would be a better fit. In fact, your experience with the asset might be the push you need to find a better friend group for yourself.